W9-DEW-764

THANKS TO MY
MOTHER

For my mother,
Raja Indurski-Weksler (1904–1974);
to whose love and bravery I owe my survival

RAJA INDURSKI-WEKSLER
VILNIUS, 1938

We remember all our foes

we commemorate all the friends

always we will link

our past with our present.

(Poem from the "Song of the Ghetto Youth" by Sz. Kaczerginski)

THANKS TO MY
MOTHER

SCHOSCHANA
RABINOVICI

TRANSLATED

FROM THE

GERMAN

BY

JAMES

SKOFIELD

DIAL BOOKS  NEW YORK

First published in the United States 1998 by Dial Books
A member of Penguin Putnam Inc.
375 Hudson Street
New York, New York 10014

Designed by Julie Rauer
Printed in the U.S.A. on acid-free paper
First Edition
3 5 7 9 10 8 6 4 2

Library of Congress Cataloging in Publication Data
Rabinovici, Schoschana, 1932–
[Dank meiner Mutter. English]
Thanks to my mother/by Schoschana Rabinovici. [translated from Hebrew
to German by Mirjam Pressler]; translated from the German by James Skofield.
p. cm.
Summary: After struggling to survive in Nazi-occupied Lithuania,
a young Jewish girl and her mother endure much suffering in Kaiserwald,
Stutthof, and Tauentzien concentration camps and on an eleven-day
death march before being liberated by the Russian army.
ISBN 0-8037-2235-4 (trade)
1. Rabinovici, Schoschana, 1932–   —Juvenile literature. 2. Jews—Persecutions—
Lithuania—Vilnius—Juvenile literature. 3. Holocaust, Jewish (1939–1945)—
Lithuania—Vilnius—Personal narratives—Juvenile literature. 4. Vilnius
(Lithuania)—Ethnic relations—Juvenile literature. [1. Rabinovici, Schoschana,
1932–   . 2. Holocaust, Jewish (1939–1945) 3. Jews—Lithuania—Vilnius.
4. Lithuania—History—German occupation, 1941–1944.]
I. Pressler, Mirjam. II. Skofield, James. III. Title.
DS135.L53R34713 1998 940.53'18'092 [B]—DC21 97-14407 CIP AC

NOTE:
The poems appearing in the text
were written by the author in the ghetto and,
especially, in the camps. They reflect the feelings and
thoughts of a literary yet unschooled child, and
were not revised in any way for this book.

MY FATHER,
ISAK WEKSLER

ON JUNE 22, 1941, I saw my father for the last time.

My parents had divorced a year before, and I had stayed with my mother.

That day there was an air-raid alert in Vilnius, a previously announced "alert drill," and the streets were empty of people. My father, a member of the civil air defense, was checking the quarter for which he was responsible. He was making sure that all the people had gone to the air-raid shelters and had blacked out their windows as required.

My father came to see me. We hadn't gone to the air-raid shelter. I sat at the window in my room, and I saw him at once. He stood next to the mailbox across from our house. I signaled him with my hand and ran downstairs. My father stood in the doorway. He hugged and kissed me, asked how I was, and said I need have no fear of the air-raid alert, and that I should be good. I wanted to go with him, but he wouldn't let me, because the all-clear hadn't sounded, and he had to return home to Grandpa Weksler, with whom he had been living since the divorce. So we said good-bye, and he promised to come again soon so that I could go visit my grandpa and play with all my cousins.

Papa

As in a dream, you move through my thoughts;
you come and blink before my eyes.
I hear your final rustle,

although you've vanished from me.
Although they robbed me of you
and left me orphaned, here.
In my heart I've shed for you
oceans of tears.
And still you stand before my eyes,
with your pale face.
Where I go and where I stay,
I hear your voice.

THE AUTHOR WITH HER PARENTS
VILNIUS, BEGINNING OF 1937

AT GRANDPA
INDURSKI'S

A YEAR AFTER THE DIVORCE, my mother, Raja
Indurski-Weksler, married Julek Rauch, a big man with a
longish face and light-brown eyes. He came from Przemyśl
in Poland, where he had attended a German school.

My parents' divorce had come after many quarrels, at
which I was often present. When there was a fight between
them, I withdrew to a corner of the dining room to watch
without them seeing me. I listened to them and was afraid.
I understood hardly a word of what they were saying, for
they deliberately spoke in Russian, but I knew my father
was furious with my mother because she had come home
too late and had met with "him" again. I didn't know *his*
name; for a long time I thought it was Jego, because when
my mother came home, my father would ask her in Russian, "Have you seen *him*?" "Him," in Russian, is *jego*. Hence
the name.

I secretly hated Jego. Without understanding how he
was involved, I was mad at him because he was the reason
for the frequent fights between my parents.

My father was a good-looking man with luxuriant
brown hair and green eyes. His right eyebrow was slightly
higher than his left, which lent his face a somewhat dubious
look although it was softened by his smile. He was only one
meter, 70 centimeters (five and a half feet) in height. But he
stood tall in my eyes, and everyone loved him because of
his good-hearted and friendly character.

My father always wore a hat with a wide brim on the

street; I loved to play with it and put it on at home. Then I'd make faces until my father laughed.

Once a strong wind blew and whisked my father's hat from his head. The hat rolled like a wheel down the littered street. Laughing, I ran after the hat, picked it up, and put it on my head. My father begged me to give it back to him, but I refused. So he went into a courtyard and waited. I went to him and gave him back the hat, and when I asked him why he hadn't run after me, he said angrily, "My head was cold. Besides, it isn't proper to walk bareheaded on the street."

I liked to sit on his knee. In the left pocket of his coat he kept a small, brown tortoiseshell comb. I sat on his knee, took out the comb, and combed his thick hair. He had beautiful, wavy hair. To this day I remember how it felt.

I loved him greatly and we were very close. We lived on Wielka Street, behind our store, Bon Ton, known throughout the city as a splendid clothes shop. Papa often took me with him for walks. In winter we went ice-skating in the park. We tied our laces together and hung the ice skates over our shoulders, and my father held my hand. I was very small, and I strained to look taller. My father skated backward on the ice, holding me by both hands and pulling me forward. Sometimes, to the sound of the music, he would dance on the ice with one of the women.

On Sundays in the spring the three of us would take a steamship ride on the Vilnya. We would get off at one of the stops along the river, walk through the meadows, and sometimes stop at a farmer's to drink a glass of fresh, warm milk that still smelled of the cow. My mother didn't care for this milk and my father would tease her about it. He and I drank the milk and ate black farmer's bread with it.

We wouldn't get home until evening, when my father would fetch goose pâté from the kosher butcher at the town hall square, and Mania, our Polish housekeeper, would serve supper.

I loved those nights. Happiness and tranquility reigned over the house. My father would put me to bed, tell me a brief story, and give me a good-night kiss. Then my parents would often go to the movies, while I stayed at home with Mania. Mania liked to sing; I would hear her beautiful voice through the open door.

My father cared about my upbringing and my manners. For Sunday lunches he often took me to a restaurant, and while we ate, he would correct my table manners.

I had a governess, Michaela, whom we called Michla, and who was responsible for my education. Sundays, in the restaurant, my father would test to see if she had taught me proper etiquette. He would order several unusual dishes to make sure that I was using the correct utensils for the course served. He taught me to eat fish with two forks. (Many years later, to the great astonishment of those around me, I would eat my fish with two forks.)

In my early years, I didn't walk correctly, and my father was anxious about my development. He took me to doctors to have my legs examined, and spent hours walking with me, during which he would correct my walk and teach me to step straight ahead and not walk pigeon-toed.

One day Michla fetched me from kindergarten. On the way home she was telling me a story and I was listening attentively to her. Suddenly someone whispered in my ear, "Devil with crooked legs." I hung my head; I knew it was my father. Once again I hadn't been walking nicely, and my father had caught me in the act.

I saw my first movies with my father. He often took me in the afternoon to the cinema, to funny films like *Dick and Doof*. My mother didn't care for such films and maintained that they would give me nightmares.

After the Russians occupied Vilnius* in 1939, my father took me to the movies two more times. I remember both films well: *The Children of Captain Grant*, based on the Jules Verne novel of the same name; and *The Last Tabor*, about a gypsy camp. Even today my memory of those two films is linked with an image of my father.

From the fall of 1939 on, when I was nearly seven, I went to school. After the start of the war I had no more governess, and so my father picked me up from school every day and took me home.

One day he came to pick me up and was sad and gloomy, which was not like him at all. I put my hand in his, and we walked side by side in silence for a long time. Suddenly he stood still, bent down to me, looked me in the eye, and said, "Susinka, I'm not going into the house with you. I'll take you only to the door. From now on I won't be living with you anymore. Soon you'll be moving to another house. Another man will be living with you. Please, never call him 'Papa.'" Tears ran from his eyes. It was the only time I saw my father cry. And thus I learned that my parents had been divorced.

Our store had been nationalized by the Russian government; when it reopened, they wouldn't let my mother set foot in it. My mother, who had worked until then in the women's clothing department, was now unemployed. Throughout this time we lived in a four-room apartment that was separated from the sales room by only a door, which was now walled up on the store side. Before that

---

* Vilnius: From 1323, the capital city of Lithuania; later, Vilnius belonged to Poland. In September of 1939 it was occupied by Soviet troops. On June 22, 1941, the Germans came into Lithuania; beginning at the end of July 1941, it gradually was incorporated into the civil administration of "Ostland," i.e., it became one part of the German-occupied territories of the Soviet Union.

happened, however, my mother managed to carry some goods from the store into our apartment.

Shortly after the loss of the store, my mother married Julek Rauch and decided to move into his large apartment, which was a few houses away on the same street. My mother began to close up our old apartment. Our house-keeper, Mania, wanted to go back to her village. Her brother had been killed in 1939, fighting against the Germans, and had left a wife and children behind. Mania wanted to help them work in the fields.

A wagon came and was loaded up with everything we wouldn't need in our new home. After many years of work-ing in the city, Mania was glad she was returning as a "rich" woman to her village, bringing money and household items. Without any prior warning, I was picked up from school one day and taken to the new apartment: Julek Rauch's apartment at Number 10, Wielka Street, first floor.

I hadn't wanted this move, and reacted by keeping silent for days. My mother, Julek, and my new sister, Dolka (Julek's daughter from his first marriage), who was about fourteen, tried to placate me. Dolka showed me the apart-ment. My new room was wonderful: large, bright, rounded on one side, and with big windows that looked out on the main street. Across the street were the splendid buildings of the main post office. My pink-colored eggshell-finish furni-ture had already been brought to the new apartment to give me the feeling that I was at home. (It had been bought by my father in Warsaw just before the start of the war, and had been a hit at the time.) The round table, the three pink chairs, and the little sofa were placed in the rounded part of the room; in a corner stood my pink bookcase with doors made of frosted red glass. In it were my toys and my books. This part of the room looked like a true small salon.

Across from the closet stood the carriage for Bébé, my big doll who really looked like a baby. In another corner of the room they had placed my pink bed and, next to it, a night table and a chest with two doors. Against the wall stood a writing desk with red plate glass on top. Overhead hung a shelf with doors made of frosted pink glass. The room was very large and light: much nicer than the one I had had in the old apartment. A door connected my room with Dolka's, which was much darker and smaller. I wondered about that, but after a while, I learned that Dolka had been persuaded to give me her nice room and move into the smaller room (where her grandmother had once lived) just so that I would feel at home.

Dolka tried to make the move easier for me, despite her opposition to the marriage and her open dislike for my mother. Her mother had left when she was just a baby, and she had been raised by her grandmother. This grandmother had died a while ago; since then Dolka had clung to her father, who was often traveling as a commercial agent. After the start of the war his business had fallen off, and he now spent most of his time at home. For Dolka he was a substitute for the dead grandmother and for the mother she had never known. Now, with her father's new marriage to a stepmother, she felt pushed aside.

My mother was a beautiful woman, one of the most beautiful women in the city. I loved and admired her greatly. She was elegantly dressed and groomed, and her appearance drew the attention of men everywhere.

She wasn't very tall; she had brown eyes, short-cropped brown hair, and delicate features. Her cheekbones were somewhat high, her nose small and straight. She had a small mouth with finely drawn lips. Her beautiful, soft hands, with their long, slender fingers and red fingernails, were especially striking. My mother wore little jewelry, but the little she did wear was exquisite. She looked fragile and behaved fastidiously, but despite that, she was a brave woman and an excellent saleswoman: smart, energetic, and very knowledgeable.

The duration of the Russian occupation of Vilnius from 1939 to 1941 passed swiftly and pleasantly for me. My mother and father vied for my love, as is often the case after a divorce. Everybody pitied me and gave me many presents, and I soon learned to exploit my situation.

Then events overtook us. At the beginning, when it was still possible to leave Vilnius and travel via Kaunas, the former capital of Lithuania, to Eretz Israel,* my father sought to obtain an immigration visa for Palestine. Two of his sisters had emigrated there before the war.

The topic led to weighty discussions. My father wanted to take me with him. He urged my mother to leave Europe with her new husband and his daughter. But even though Julek's family had already been living in Brazil for a long time, Julek emphatically refused to leave Poland. He was a fiery Polish patriot; he believed the war would end soon, and he wanted to work to help build a free Polish state in which we could live in peace, as before. When my father finally obtained the desired papers, my mother flat-out refused to part with me.

My father, who loved my mother despite everything, had agreed at the divorce to leave me with her—first, because she had insisted, and he was used to giving in to her; and second, because he himself had grown up without a mother. His mother had died in childbirth, and he had had a stepmother. He wanted to spare me a similar fate. This sacrifice was to condemn him. My mother wouldn't give me up, and he hesitated to go without me.

When he finally decided to leave, it was too late. Only

* Eretz Israel was the name used by the Jews of the Diaspora for what was then called Palestine.

the first group had succeeded in leaving Kaunas. The second group was detained by the Russian authorities.

In 1941 the Russians began to deport Vilnius' rich townspeople to forced labor in Siberia. My mother's family, the Indurskis, was well-to-do and on the blacklist. My father's family, the Wekslers, although also rich townspeople, were allowed to stay in Vilnius because the workers at their candy factory intervened for them.

Grandfather Weksler still headed the company, although now as a salaried director, and my father was also able to continue his work as a technical advisor, a job he loved greatly.

Julek had influential friends. He sought to delay the deportation of Grandfather Indurski and his family, because my mother was also on the list. The whole business took a long while; in the meantime we waited with packed bags, ready to be displaced. Then, at the last minute, and by paying a lot of money, Julek was able to get us crossed off the deportation list. There were three deportations sent from Vilnius to Siberia, and we were among the lucky ones who succeeded in buying their freedom.

Then suddenly, in June 1941, the Germans occupied Vilnius, two days after they had invaded the Soviet Union.

I sat with Dolka on the big windowsill in my room. We looked out and saw the soldiers of the German army enter the city.

It was a sad day. The streets were deserted. Most people were afraid and stayed at home. Members of the fascistic Lithuanian police, who had been replaced in the previous year by the Russian police, now came out of hiding. They patrolled the streets and helped the German army to maintain "order." They lent special assistance in pursuing and fighting the Russian forces. With our own eyes Dolka and I saw the Lithuanian police occupy the post office across the street.

My mother and Julek wouldn't allow us to remain seated at the window. They closed the window and pulled the blinds down just as they would have during a blackout.

Suddenly, heavy blows were heard on our door, and then there was shouting in German: "Open up! Hurry up, hurry up!"

We were terrified. We feared they might have come because of Julek. At that time we still thought only men were being taken. Julek hid in a closet in the bedroom, and our old housekeeper opened the door.

German soldiers swarmed inside. The old woman was pushed aside and fell to the floor. The men, a few officers among them, climbed over her without paying any attention. The house caretaker followed them. Without saying a word, the soldiers stormed from room to room and halted only when they came to the big living room. There a great big officer, standing with his legs wide apart, barked at the caretaker in German that he was to make sure the apartment was cleared out within twenty-four hours. All the furniture was to remain. The old Pole didn't understand; he tried to ask questions, but the big officer was already gone, and the soldier who followed him out struck the caretaker on the head with his rifle butt. As swiftly as they had come, the soldiers disappeared and left the old man behind, lying in his own blood.

The sound of their boots was still ringing in the stairwell as my mother closed the apartment door and helped the old housekeeper to her feet. Dolka brought water and a handkerchief for the caretaker, but he didn't want her help. He hissed out a hate-filled "Żydówka"—"Jewess." Dolka was hurt and frightened and began to cry. She had lived in the house for years and up to then had considered the caretaker to be a good friend. When she started to cry, Julek came out of the closet, for he was afraid his daughter had been injured. Julek, who spoke fluent German, was the only one who had understood the commands of the officer; in the ensuing hubbub, he tried to explain what the German officer had demanded.

Fearful, I shrank back into the corner by the sofa and tried to make myself as small as possible.

My mother soon collected herself. In a loud voice she suggested, "Let's have a cup of tea." The housekeeper went into the kitchen to prepare tea and cookies. When all four of us were seated at the table, Julek said, "What will we do? Where will we go?"

My mother had already decided: We would go to her father, who lived a few houses down at Number 1, Samkowa Street.

After we had finished drinking our tea, my mother arranged for the housekeeper, Dolka, and Julek to pack all the most important and necessary things in suitcases. Everything that wouldn't fit in the suitcases would be packed into bedsheets. My mother set off for Grandfather's, carrying the first bundle.

After a while other members of the family arrived: my mother's sister Julia, with her husband, Jechiel; my mother's brother, Wolodja, with his wife, Chassia, and my grandfather, too. My mother ordered me to stow my doll, Bébé, and all the toys I especially loved, in my big doll carriage. I put my books in a knapsack that my grandfather carried to his house.

Before we left the house, my mother said I should sit down in the chair next to the door. I sat there a couple of minutes. This was the custom in my family, when leaving the house for any length of time. It was supposed to bring good luck.

Together with Grandfather I left the apartment. I pushed the full doll carriage. We went along Wielka Street, crossed the next street, and came to the house where Grandfather lived. There were few people on the street, and we took care not to draw attention to ourselves. We stepped quickly through the building door and went up the back stairs to Grandfather's apartment, so that the neighbors wouldn't notice we were moving in. Thus, almost in secret, we made it to Grandfather's apartment. During the day the adults had constantly run back and forth, carrying our clothes and our other things. These now lay in bundles and packets, in a heap, in one of the small rooms that had been put at our disposal.

Before my mother and Julek left our apartment, German officers arrived and carefully checked that everything was neat and clean and, especially, that no furniture or kitchen utensils were missing. Finally, they installed a new lock and pasted a notice to the door: "Confiscated."

Grandfather's apartment had many rooms, but now almost the entire family was living with him. At the outbreak of war in 1939 Julia and Jechiel and their daughter, Jochele, had moved in. Jechiel Tejschew was a professional farmer, an unusual occupation for a young Jew at that time. He had worked as a farmer his whole life, and after his marriage to my aunt Julia he had rented a farm, Puszkarnia. Youth groups of the Zionist* movement, who were preparing to emigrate to Palestine, often came to him to learn about farming.

The young couple moved into a big house, the former manor of the farm family, and Jechiel was in charge of running the farm. We children of the family had always spent our summer vacations at Puszkarnia.

I remember how he and his farmers brought produce into town. Mornings, the freshest vegetables were always loaded onto a wagon and driven to the big market of Vilnius; Jechiel sat up on top by the driver. When he returned

---

* Zionism: A Jewish movement that originated at the end of the nineteenth century, with the goal of creating a Jewish state in Palestine.

about midday, he brought us many presents and sweets from the city. He was a pleasant and quiet man who loved children greatly. He often played ball with us. We enjoyed those summertimes.

Year after year planning for the summer holidays began early in the season. Clothing and toys would be packed, even pots and dishes, and one day a farmer with a great two-harness rack wagon would appear. He would load the luggage on the wagon. We sat up on top of the heap: the family children, with our nannies and governesses. Happy and joyful, we would arrive in Puszkarnia.

We swam in the river that flowed through the countryside. We climbed trees, played with the farm children, and ran through the meadows. We ate vegetables that had just been picked and washed in huge buckets. We drank fresh new milk, and went to the chicken coop to collect eggs for breakfast. The farmers were friendly with us and often invited us to their huts to eat potatoes and a delicious cabbage soup.

My uncle Jechiel, a tall, broad-shouldered man, more resembled one of the farmers of his property than he did our family. He had reddish hair, a round, fleshy face burned red by the sun, and small blue eyes. His eyebrows and lashes were so fair, you almost could not see them. His hands were broad and short, very strong and accustomed to farmwork.

In summertime he mostly stayed at Puszkarnia; only in winter did he come back to the city. His wife, Julia, tall and very slender, with a long face and curly light-brown hair, was the exact opposite of her husband. She was delicate, quiet, and very serious. I can't remember ever seeing her smile and only seldom recall her singing lullabies to Jochele. She had a lovely, expressive voice.

When the Jewish holy days approached in the autumn, she left Puszkarnia with her little daughter and returned to

Grandfather, moving into two of the small bedrooms in the back of his apartment. She stayed there until Easter, and her husband came to visit her from time to time.

Jochele was Julia and Jechiel's only child, a sweet girl, little and chubby, with blond curls. She was two years younger than I.

Grandmother had died in 1938. Since then, Julia had cared for Grandfather and taken charge of his household.

My grandfather Schmarjahu Indurski was a small, spare man with a bald head. He had a shiny, long face, with big gray-green eyes, a short beard, and a back bent from hard work. He was the oldest son of a poor family that was rich with offspring. He had lost his father when still quite young. He left school and apprenticed to a glovemaker—a profession common among the Jews of Vilnius—to earn an income for his mother and his siblings. Later he met a beautiful and rich girl from a good and cultivated household, the youngest daughter of Welwel Schochot, a feldscher.* They married.

Grandfather's home was very large. It was in a house in the middle of the city: at the end of Wielka Street and the beginning of Samkowa Street, right across from the main entrance of the university. On the ground floor of the house were a few shops. One of them, a shop for leather gloves, belonged to my grandfather; another was a café, the pastry shop Strahl (ray). Over the entrance to Grandfather's shop hung a gilded iron glove and a sign: "Indurski Gloves." Over the door to the pastry shop hung a giant, green-painted, cast-iron hand holding a burning torch. This pastry shop was called The Green Ray, to distinguish it from The Red Ray, the Mizkewicza—another branch of the pastry shop, located on the main street.

From the front courtyard (many of Vilnius' houses had

---

* Feldscher: A low-ranking military surgeon.

a front *and* a back courtyard), a broad, ornate marble staircase led up to Grandfather's apartment. This was on the second floor. The Strahl family lived in the apartment just across the way. They were devout Catholics, the proprietors of the pastry shops, and owners of the building. There were very good relations between the two families. The children played together in the courtyard and were invited over for parties and holidays.

A dark, narrow stairwell led from the courtyard to the back entrances of the apartments. The steps were made of cast iron and were taller than usual. We children were forbidden to use these steps lest we stumble in the dark and fall down them.

From the back steps (the "black entrance," as we called it in Polish), one entered the roomy kitchen. From it one door led to the housekeeper's small room; another led to the dining room, a big room with a table around whose expanse the entire family could sit down at mealtimes. From the dining room one entered a very large room, the parlor. After the death of Grandmother, Grandfather had set up his bed in this room, the center of the apartment. It now served half the time as bedroom, half the time as living room. In the long days following, when we weren't allowed to go out, we children played—as if we were living in a forest—among the flowerpots that stood in front of the high windows. The living room had two more doors: one to the corridor leading to the front entrance, and another to a very small room. From there one passed on to more rooms arranged in a row—five small bedrooms, one after the other. At the very end there was a big, beautiful bathroom, with a second door to the corridor near the house door. The apartment was certainly big, but it had never been intended to accommodate several families.

We got two of the small bedrooms: one for Julek and my mother, the second for Dolka and me. Julia, Jechiel, and

Jochele had to walk through our rooms every time they wanted to get to their bedrooms, which were behind ours. For the first time our living situation became narrow and uncomfortable. Still, my mother tried to make our life as pleasant as possible. Most of what we had hastily brought with us from our apartment still lay tied up in the bed-sheets. On some of these soft bundles my mother laid the mattresses, and so our beds were very high. I used to pretend I was up on a high mountain, because I saw only sky through the upper, unobstructed part of the window.

My mother was able to get in touch with both of the young women who had previously worked in our store, and whom she thought trustworthy: pretty, blond Vera, and Olga, who was darker and a bit older. They came to us at Grandfather's apartment, and my mother shut herself up in her room with them and spoke with them a long time. After a while the young women went away, loaded down with bundles—a part of the goods my mother had earlier rescued from the store.

They came a few more times. In this manner most of the new things in the apartment were taken to the homes of the two Polish women, and my mother and Julek had more space in their room, which had looked like a storeroom before. Naturally, my mother hoped by doing this to safeguard those things that could be sold or traded for food if it became necessary.

Difficult times had begun for the Jews of Vilnius. The Germans gave orders that we would all have to wear a yellow star on our outer clothes. Yellow material was obtained, and Grandfather went into his old workroom, in which he had worked his entire life cutting out gloves, and cut and stitched yellow stars for the whole family. Mother and Julia fastened them to the chests and backs of our garments.

It was a sad day. We children crowded together into the

bathroom so we wouldn't disturb the adults at their shameful work. We sat there and looked out the little window that opened on a side street off Wielka Street.

Suddenly two men with yellow stars ran past our house, followed closely by Lithuanian policemen. We opened the window, leaned on the windowsill, and looked out. Suddenly we heard shouting in Polish and Lithuanian, and, repeatedly, the word "Żyd," Jew. The policemen caught both men and led them away. The Jews, with their arms raised, were shoved forward, and the policemen struck their backs with their rifle butts.

More and more pursuers appeared, policemen and "chappers" (catchers). They hunted down people wearing yellow stars. Casual passersby stopped and watched the drama disinterestedly. The windows of surrounding houses were opened, and people looked out and listened to the clamor.

We children ran to our parents and told them what we had seen. The adults opened a larger window and looked out. But when they heard the shouts of "Żyd, Żyd!" they quickly closed all the windows and pulled the heavy drapes over them. It grew dark in all the bedrooms.

What we children had seen was the start of the "catches."

The chappers were shock troops made up of Lithuanian youths and students, who had voluntarily signed up to fight against the Jews. These troops were often dressed as civilians, but were mostly recognizable by their black-leather jackets. At their head was Martin Weiss, the boss of the Gestapo.

The chappers persecuted Jews. They arrested primarily men and took them to Lukiszki Prison. At that time we still thought that Jewish men were being arrested to be sent to a work camp.

Many Jews who were employed by the German authorities had a pass, a work permit. They came home in the evening; but all those caught by the chappers never returned.

On July 13, 1941, Gestapo trucks drove through the streets of the city and stopped in front of buildings in which Jews lived. The chappers broke into the homes and ordered all the men to get dressed, get soap and towels, and come with them. They calmed the terrified women with the explanation that their men were being sent to work. That day two thousand men were taken to Lukiszki. The chappers had "cleansed" whole streets.

My uncle Maisiei Nowogródzki was one of those taken away. The chappers broke into his home on Subocz Street, and he wasn't able to hide in time. He didn't resist, because he thought it was futile. Before he left, he kissed his wife, hugged his daughter and kissed her, too, and said, "Mind your mama, and stay with her always."

Maisiei was the uncle I loved most, a spiritual, quiet, and unassuming man. He worked as a high-ranking clerk for a Jewish bank in Vilnius and commanded great respect. When he married Lena, Mother's oldest sister, they set up housekeeping in a rented four-room apartment with a view of the small Wilenka River, not far from the bank.

Their apartment was beautiful; besides the adults' room and that of Lea, their only daughter, there was also a room full of books, the library. There, Maisiei, dressed in dark clothes and a dark tie, thick glasses on his nose, sat behind his writing desk and read one of his many books. His thin black hair was always combed neatly; his gaze was wise and inquisitive. He was the soul of quiet and goodness and lent composure and security to his surroundings. He had a quiet manner of speaking, persuasive and reliable. He often read us folktales or told us the most interesting and beautiful fairy tales. I loved to visit him. I soaked up his stories, and later, at home, I'd tell them to myself again and again.

Maisiei came from a working-class Jewish family and was raised amid Vilnius' Jewish labor movement. I don't know whether he belonged to any party. Nevertheless, he often used to involve the older members of the family in political discussions.

Sometimes people came to visit Maisiei, and together they would shut themselves up in his study and have long talks. He was a Yiddishist. That meant he loved and studied the Yiddish language, and often wrote things down in one of his thick notebooks.

His wife, Lena, a cool, quiet woman, also always had a book in her hand or else was playing the piano. Lena was sickly and weak, and the whole family treated her gingerly. Her features were very soft, and her skin so pale it gave the impression of being transparent. She looked like the porcelain doll that presided over the dining room's sideboard. Although I didn't know then that her name, Helena, meant "little hen" in its Yiddish form ("Hindl"), she always reminded me of a cuckoo or a small bird.

Their daughter, Lea, was six years older than I. She was a merry, pleasant girl with thick, wavy brown hair. She was enterprising and cultivated and studied hard, hitting the schoolbooks even in her free time. I liked her very much. I had learned a lot from her and made an effort to be like her.

When her father was taken away, Lea packed up their essentials, closed their apartment, and came to Grandfather's with her mother. It was a long way. Jews were forbidden to use the major streets of Vilnius, and a couple of times they met chappers on the side streets. When they arrived, Lea was upset by the sight of the full apartment. But Aunt Julia took Jochele into her room, and so a bedroom was freed up.

At Grandfather's, Lea treated her mother as if she were her daughter. She cared for her and protected her from any excitement.

The danger posed by the chappers grew. More and more frequently we could hear screams and running footsteps. The
chappers forced their way into Jewish homes and took the
men away with them. Out of fear of them, it was decided
that my mother's younger brother, Wolodja, would have to
come with his family and sleep at Grandfather's home.
Wolodja, his wife, Chassia, and their little daughter, Fejgele,
lived in a smaller apartment off the same courtyard, across
from us.

CHASSIA AND FEJGELE,
SUMMER 1939

Dolka and I were moved into the bathroom. In it was a white couch on which Grandfather used to rest after his bath. My mother made up a bed for me on this couch, and Dolka slept on a mattress on the floor.

The apartment was now full to bursting with bundles, clothes, and people. Most of the time everyone stayed inside. From six at night until six in the morning there was a curfew imposed on Jews. Furthermore, they were forbidden to listen to the news, and so the stróż, the building caretaker, took away our radio.

The food provisions were insufficient for so many people, but our Polish neighbors, the Strahls, demonstrated their friendship during the emergency. From time to time they brought us food that they bought for us in the shop. Moreover, they invited us children to play in their apartment and the adults to come listen to the news on the radio.

The news was very depressing. The retreat of the Russians had released a wave of refugees. Many young Socialists, Communists, and Jews had left the city for the Soviet Union, but most of them, including many Jews, didn't make it there. They fell into the hands of the advancing German army, or they were killed by Lithuanians who had joined the German soldiers in pursuit of the Soviet army. There were rumors of friends and acquaintances who had fled with the Russian army, and of others who had been killed while they were fleeing. I feared for my father, because he no longer came to visit. Was it possible he had fled with the Russians? If so, then it was certainly very dangerous. But no one could answer my questions; even my mother knew nothing.

One day Uncle Schneior, my father's younger brother, came to us and told us what had happened on June 25, the first day of the German occupation of Vilnius. My father had returned home to Grandfather Weksler. But before he had gone up to the apartment, he had stood at the door for a moment. German soldiers were marching through the streets, and the Polish caretaker, an old man and an anti-Semite, greeted the Germans with great enthusiasm. When he noticed my father, he called loudly, "Bow down to the Germans, Jew!"

Alarmed, my father looked at him, but a German officer who happened to be passing just then approached and said, "Jews don't need to bow before Germans." Then he ordered my father to accompany him. My father was taken to the city prison, Lukiszki, and nobody had heard any more about him from that time on.

At the time I was glad, because I thought at least he wouldn't be killed like those who had attempted to flee before the advance of the German soldiers.

Later I learned that on July 4 the first Jews had been murdered in Ponary, a suburb of Vilnius. They had been taken there from Lukiszki Prison. From then until July 20th, about five thousand Jewish men were murdered in Ponary.

A Bright Summer Day

It was a bright summer day,
the sun warmed the earth,
the world laughed, dressed up, and enjoyed itself.
Only with me, the cold remains,
the streets are all deserted;
no people can be seen.
I sit at the window and think,
and wish for the day to pass quickly,
and fear what the night will bring.
The night did not bring me
tidings and sadness,
but the bright day.
I sit and I wait,
and see in the distance

a man who comes toward me
from the street corner.
He comes up to me
and tells me the news:
For we Jews the suffering now begins.
The Germans have come to Vilnius.
And they've brought worry with them.
Your Father was standing before a small door
when a uniformed man approached him.
The janitor said: That's a Jew.
We don't need Jews, I'll take him along.
Said and done, at a stroke,
your father is locked
behind prison walls.
When he'll come back, and what happens next,
you, my child, will soon understand for yourself.
With time, you will know, in wretched misery,
that your father is gone to his death,
and was taken away from you
by a man in German uniform.
I didn't answer a single word,
as you will surely understand;
I only began to weep.

One day the chappers came to us, too. They banged loudly on the outer door. Panic seized us.

Before the housekeeper opened the door, we children were sent into the bathroom. There we sat, trembling with fear and listening to the racket outside. The chappers rushed into the apartment and ran from room to room, looking for men. But this time it was a blessing that the apartment was built like a train, one room after another.

Julek, Jechiel, and Wolodja succeeded in getting through the rooms to the kitchen, and then they disappeared quietly into the back stairwell. Our neighbors' door opened suddenly in front of them, and old Mrs. Strahl beckoned them to come into her apartment.

The chappers raged through our place. They opened the bundles and threw all the contents about; they smashed dishes and toppled flowerpots and chairs. They shouted and demanded someone tell them where the men were.

The women huddled in the corners of the rooms, and only Grandfather stayed seated at his place at the big dining table. With one of the heavy objects lying around, one of the intruders struck Grandfather and pushed over his chair. Grandfather fell under the table and lay there, blood streaming all over him.

The assault lasted only a few minutes. The chappers stormed through the apartment and disappeared through the back door. We could hear their footsteps drumming against the iron steps; then the shouts faded into the distance. It grew quiet.

Little by little the women stirred and came out of their corners. The apartment looked like the aftermath of a pogrom.* All the women first ran to the bathroom to see how we were. When they were certain that nothing had happened to the children, they began to look for the men. But it was as though the earth had swallowed them up.

Then they found Grandfather, wounded, under the dining table. He said that Wolodja, Julek, and Jechiel had fled through the back door. Perhaps they had hidden in the attic.

Lena looked after Grandfather; Chassia stayed with us. My mother and Julia ran out to look for the men: Julia through the front door, my mother through the back door. She was already in the stairwell when the Strahls' rear apartment door opened suddenly, and Mrs. Strahl signaled my mother that the men were with her. Only when it was

---

* Pogrom (Russian for "devastation"): Term for the persecution, with violence and plunder, of a specific group of people, especially Jews.

certain that the chappers had left the courtyard did Julek, Jechiel, and Wolodja return to us.

We felt deep admiration for the humane old lady who had placed herself in danger in order to afford a refuge to persecuted Jews.

From that day on—a day full of fear and panic—we children stopped playing. I believe we even stopped singing. There were five of us: two-year-old Fejgele; six-year-old Jochele; I, the eight-year-old; Lea, the fourteen-year-old; and Dolka, who was already sixteen. We sat there quietly. We withdrew into ourselves, and I held my doll in my arms. We sat in that bathroom as if we were in a bunker; only at mealtimes did we leave our hiding place and sit at the dining table with the adults.

The household was on constant alert. The men readied hiding places for themselves: in the attic, in the cellar, and in the closets of the apartment. We all stood watch. When chappers appeared in the side streets or in the courtyard, the men hid immediately. Grandfather remained pale and still; I often saw him crying.

Once Wolodja went down to his own apartment to get something for his daughter. He was scared by what met his eyes. The door was broken down, and many things had disappeared. Everything that remained was smashed and jumbled. The neighbors, who didn't know where Wolodja and his family were, had stolen furniture and other household items.

At the beginning of September we heard a new word: "provocation." The adults were very upset and bewildered by it. We children knew that something bad had happened, but it took a while before we had an idea what provocation meant—namely, "false accusation." For example, a rumor was spread about that a Jew had shot a German and wounded him. Immediately, pogroms started up.

The next day the following notice was posted on the

walls of the houses: "On Sunday three Germans were killed by Jews; the murderers were arrested and shot. In order to deter further such crimes, a ban will be imposed on being outdoors between the hours of 3:00 P.M. and 10:00 A.M."

The night before this announcement the old streets of the Jewish quarter were sealed off. Historically, Vilnius' old ghetto was comprised of Gaon Street, Gleser Street, Jatkever Lane, and Hospital Street. Many Jews lived there.

That night the Germans stormed into each house, into all the attics and into each cellar, and dragged everyone out: women, men, and children. The streets were coated with blood, and corpses lay everywhere. About five thousand Jews were taken to Ponary; by the next day their homes had already been plundered.

We learned of the murders, as did Jews in other parts of the city. Fear, pain, and despair were widespread. But that wasn't the end of it; new ordinances hostile to Jews broke over our heads. The seizure of Jewish property had begun. A "contribution" was imposed on the Jews of Vilnius, which meant they had to pay a heavy fine. Acquaintances came to take away our portion of the contribution.

On the morning of September 6, notice was given that all Jews would have to leave their homes. They had to pack the possessions they could carry and move to the ghetto. This measure wasn't unexpected; we knew that the Germans had set up ghettos in other cities and had concentrated all the Jews there. A few days earlier my grandfather had already gathered all his belongings: gold coins, jewelry, and everything else of value he owned. That evening, together with Wolodja, he had secretly left the apartment.

They went to the cellar of the building, where every tenant had a separate cubicle that could be locked up. Wolodja moved aside a few boxes containing stuff Grandfather had stored when his shop had been shut down. Then he began to dig a deep hole in the hard-packed earth. The work was difficult, because it was cramped and dark, and they didn't turn on the light for safety's sake. Moreover, the work had to be done quietly, so as not to attract the attention of the caretaker and the other neighbors. In our apartment above, the adults sat, drinking tea and waiting, after they had put us children to bed.

Night came, but they didn't return. A tense atmosphere, full of fear and worry, dominated the apartment. Chassia was crying and berating herself because she had let Wolodja go with Grandfather. Even then, it had become clear to all that neither one's own life nor another's should be risked just to save a few valuables. The adults sat around the table the whole night and waited.

Wolodja and Grandfather had stayed in the cellar. First they had dug a hole and buried a portion of the coins and all the jewelry. Then they had shoved the storage boxes back over the hole and rearranged them to show no trace of their work. Finally, they dug a second hole and put the remaining coins in it.

When they had gone down to the cellar, it had already been dark, and they knew, because they had left the apartment after curfew, that they were already in danger. Since they had finished their work late at night, they decided to stay in the cellar, and not risk crossing the courtyard and climbing the stairs again. It wasn't only dangerous because they might be caught outside during curfew. Someone might also get ideas as to why they had gone to the cellar; then all their exertions would have been for nothing. Therefore, the whole night through, they sat in the dark, in the cellar, crouching among the boxes.

The next morning, when the courtyard began its usual stir, and the workers at the pastry shop appeared, they left the cellar secretly and climbed up the back stairs to the apartment.

Everyone waiting breathed easier when they opened the

door. They embraced one another, kissing and crying by turns. We children were wakened by the noise. We went to the dining room, saw it all, and understood none of it.

The news about the approaching removal of Jewish families to the ghetto had circulated to Jews of surrounding towns and villages, and also reached Mania's village. One morning she arrived, driving a wagon pulled by two nags. Good, loyal Mania brought us bread, milk, butter, cheese, eggs, and meat from the village, and—especially for Grandfather—a live hen,* because she knew he ate only kosher meat.

We were glad to see her. We hugged and kissed her, and she stayed with us the whole day. Before she departed, my mother loaded her wagon up with household items and all manner of things that we couldn't take with us when we left. Mania took all these things and promised to stay in touch, and to visit us as often as she possibly could.

---

* The hen had to be living because, in keeping with Jewish dietary laws, it would have to be ritually slaughtered.

29

THE
VILNIUS GHETTO

VEHICLES WITH LOUDSPEAKERS drove through the city and announced that on the following day, all Jews would be taken to the ghetto. In our part of the city, there was almost no contact any longer among the isolated Jewish families; most sat in their homes and feared to go out into the streets. We didn't know whom we could ask for advice, or what we should do. After the loudspeakers had announced the bad news, we immediately began to prepare for the move. We had neither the time nor the opportunity to retrieve Grandfather's valuables, but a short while earlier my mother had hidden all her jewelry, her money, and her gold coins in our clothes. She had sewn her jewelry and coins into her coat, into the fur collar of my coat, into the hem of Dolka's coat, and into the shoulder pads of Julek's coat. Now we went into our rooms and started to pack.

Since we didn't know whether we would be able to get anything later, we decided to pack the most essential things first. A few articles of clothing for each of us, sheets, handkerchiefs, soap, and food, so that we would at least have something to eat for the first few days. We also packed pots and dishes and prepared a few bundles in case we were able to return and retrieve some things. After the plunder of Wolodja's apartment, we reasoned that most of the neighbors and the employees of the pastry shop wouldn't be able to pass up the opportunity to plunder the vacated apartment. Still, we hoped to be able to rescue some of our things.

We entrusted the valuable things from Grandfather's apartment to our good neighbors, the Strahl family. In an emergency, we hoped, we could sell some of those things or trade them for food.

For us—that is, for Mama, Julek, Dolka, and me—it was the second time within two months that we were forced to change homes. It was as Grandfather always said: "To move twice is like being burned down once."

Our possessions, at any rate, were greatly diminished. Little remained to Lena and Lea either; they hadn't gone back to their apartment and didn't know if it even existed any longer. Wolodja's things had been mostly plundered or wrecked; he possessed only the things he was wearing.

But it was hardest for Grandfather.

This was his home. He had established it, and had cared for it his whole life. Here he and his beloved wife had raised their children; here they had married; and here his grandchildren had visited him.

Everything in the apartment was bound up with memories. He possessed precious books, various religious articles needed for his daily observances, silver and porcelain; all the things that belonged to his life. He was seventy years old, and a life full of work lay behind him. He had been so proud of what he had attained: of his home; of his store, the glove shop he had built up with his own hands; of the good reputation he had earned. Out of all that, only his home remained; now he would have to leave it, too.

His daughters helped him with the packing; again and again there were conflicts. Grandfather would have preferred taking everything with him, but the old man could carry no heavy bundle on his back. Therefore, his daughters advised him to pack only his personal necessities, and to abandon all his keepsakes: the photographs, the presents and souvenirs, all the things that had been vital parts of his life. With each thing that had to be left behind, he crumpled a bit more. So Wolodja arranged for a small cart to be loaded with Grandfather's most personal possessions; that way he could take a bit more with him than he could have carried.

Next morning, after a sleepless night, we were ready to go. Grandfather said, "Let's drink a glass of tea."

This was a family custom. The old maid started the samovar and laid the table with the good china. We all sat down at the table, each at his usual place. Maisiei's place was empty.

Lea, his oldest grandchild, sat to Grandfather's right; I sat to his left. He held my hand. Quietly, without speaking, we drank our tea. Then we all said good-bye to the old maid. Grandfather paid her salary through the end of the year, and made her a gift of some things. He cared for this woman as a daughter.

We placed a few seats by the entrance door. When we heard the sound of the loudspeakers in the courtyard, ordering the Jews to leave their houses and come out, each of us took his pack, and went to the door. Here we put down our things and sat down on the seats, one family after the other, as was usual with us before a long journey. After a short time we stood up, took our things, and went down. We now said good-bye to the Strahl family. The other neighbors didn't bother to open their doors to wish us a safe return. But we knew some of them were standing behind their closed doors and eavesdropping. We sensed who was troubled and sad, and who was merely waiting impatiently for us to be gone so they could go and ransack Grandfather's apartment.

Now we were on our way to the ghetto.

We stood in the courtyard. Each of us carried a big bundle on his back and other baggage in his hands. The Lithuanian police went from house to house and assembled the groups to be taken, under guard, to the ghetto.

When the police arrived at our house, my grandfather stood at the head of our group, and the big bundle on his bent back covered him almost completely. His small figure, always stooped, bent over even deeper, but he didn't collapse, and he was the first to leave the courtyard of his home, followed by the rest of his family. Chassia pushed the baby carriage and Fejgele sat on top of the baggage.

I found myself at the rear. I carried a full knapsack on my back, and I pushed my big doll carriage, which was crammed. This time, except for the doll, there were no toys in it; my mother had loaded my doll carriage with my clothes and essential household items.

My mother carried a bundle on her back, things tied up in a bedsheet. She also carried two big suitcases in her hands. She walked next to me. Julek and Dolka walked at the end of the sad procession. Dolka carried heavy packages and Julek pulled a handcart with mattresses for the whole family. Besides that he carried a big bundle on his back.

Despite the shouts of the police who were urging us on, we moved forward slowly. We crossed Wielka Street and then took a left turn into a side street, in the direction of the university. We passed the gates of the university on our right, and went on, to the old Jewish quarter. This oldest part of the city, whose previous Jewish inhabitants had been removed earlier, had been cleared by the Germans of its Christian inhabitants the night before. They closed the whole quarter and built walls in nearly all the passages, leaving some gates for transit. In this way they had established a ghetto, which was named Ghetto 2, to differentiate it from the big, central Ghetto 1.

It was a small quarter, between three alleys: Gleser Street, Yiddish Alley, and Jatkever Lane. It extended as far as the house of the Gaon of Vilnius.* Eleven thousand people were crammed into this quarter.

I don't know how it happened, but we immediately secured a small, empty apartment in one of the houses. We stood, depressed, in the doorway. The apartment still seemed alive. The previous inhabitants must have left only a short time before. They had left a great mess behind. Photographs, books, torn letters, and clothes lay on the floor; the beds hadn't been made; and the remains of a meal were still on the table.

The apartment consisted of four minute rooms and a toilet, which was a rarity in this old quarter. To our joy, there was even running water in the kitchen.

Grandfather, Lena, and Lea set themselves up in the rearmost room; Jechiel, Julia, and Jochele in the second room; and we took the big middle room. Wolodja, Chassia, and Fejgele moved into the small room next to the kitchen and toilet.

We were among the lucky few that day. Sixty thousand people were rounded up into both ghettos. Circumstances were so straitened that many people who couldn't find room in houses had to sleep outdoors, in entranceways or next to walls.

It was pure chance that we had wound up in Ghetto 2. That was determined by where one had lived in Vilnius, and by the arbitrariness of the Lithuanian police. We didn't know—couldn't even know—of the differences that would emerge between the two ghettos in time. Therefore, we also didn't know which of the two was more advantageous. We settled down in our new apartment and were relieved that we at least had a roof over our heads.

The housing shortage in the ghetto was difficult to en-

---

* Gaon of Vilnius: Rabbi Elijah ben Solomon Zalmen, a renowned and esteemed intellectual and Talmudic scholar of the eighteenth century.

dure. Every place, every crack, every nook was taken. Many people lay on their bundles on the pavement, and in the courtyards, exhausted, hungry, and depressed. Everyone was looking for space; we had to guard our apartment from the poorest, who tried to force their way in and settle down with us. Many people slept in the synagogues, in schools, in public bathhouses and in the other public spaces of the old ghetto.

By order of the Germans a Jewish ghetto police force was established. At night this police force had to round up all the people who were sleeping outside in the open air. These people had to be turned over to the German authorities, or else the whole ghetto would suffer the penalties. Only six days after our arrival in the ghetto, on September 12, we learned that over three thousand Jews had already been rounded up and taken to Ponary. Again and again we heard of the murders in Ponary, but we still didn't believe it.

Ghetto 1 was designated by the Germans as the ghetto for tradesmen and skilled workers. Ghetto 2 would be predominantly for old and sick people, people who didn't engage in a trade, merchants, and intellectuals. The majority of them would not be assigned work; they would receive no food rations, and no pass that permitted them to work. The pass really meant permission to live. The inhabitants of Ghetto 2 lived in fear, in anticipation, and with constant strain on their nerves. They were depressed, afflicted, and in horror of the "actions." Because they had no passes, they envied the inhabitants of Ghetto 1. The organization of food distribution progressed slowly in Ghetto 2, and the food that was distributed was inadequate for so many people. From the first day on, people were stalked by hunger.

On Fridays my grandfather always prayed in a small prayer house in the courtyard of the Schul-Hojf Synagogue. It was a large courtyard. For hundreds of years it had contained small prayer houses as well as the big mikva, the religious bath, and other religious establishments. The poor of the city used to beg for alms there, and those who had no roof over their heads could sleep in one of its many entranceways. The insane of the city hung about, and there was also a soup kitchen for the poor. From there, my grandfather brought home news of the ghetto's mood.

Time passed, and the Jewish holy days arrived. Rosh Hashanah* was sad; we sat on the mattresses we had brought to the ghetto with us; we hadn't a dining table. Wolodja had succeeded in obtaining some boards. From them, he built a poor table. Only four people could sit around it. We also lacked chairs, and so we ate the meager meal prepared in honor of the holiday—my grandfather and the men sitting about the table, and we women and children sitting on the mattresses against the wall. After the meal we wished one another a good new year. It was very sad.

On the evening of Yom Kippur** the first big "action" began.

German soldiers, and their Lithuanian accomplices, forced their way into the ghetto. They went from building to building and ordered the inhabitants to come out of their apartments and assemble outside. In our building many families obeyed the orders, but we had decided to remain inside.

My grandfather had told us a strange story. The evening before the holiday, he had met the Balebessl*** of Vilnius. He and his multitudinous family had lived their whole lives

---

* Rosh Hashanah: The Jewish New Year's celebration that usually falls in September or October.
** Yom Kippur: The day of atonement; a day of repentance and reconciliation observed with fasting and prayers.
*** Popular designation for a rabbi who is said to be able to foretell the future.

here in the district of the present-day ghetto. My grandfather had stopped to converse with this man. He had questioned him about his opinion of the situation, and—because of the man's foresight—had asked him how we should fare in the future. The Balebessl of Vilnius recommended Grandfather hide during the next few days. He shouldn't walk the streets, nor should he give himself up to the Germans. He said that Grandfather should stay at home with his whole family during the "action" that would take place in the next few days. My grandfather hadn't understood what the Balebessl of Vilnius meant, and the Balebessl hadn't explained it to him.

Grandfather asked him if he would do the same. The man said, "No, I will not hide. It wouldn't help me. Death awaits me in a few days, and my whole family will die with me. I am sorry about my children, but this is my fate, and I and my whole family will go and give ourselves up to the enemy. But you must hide yourself; think it over."

When Grandfather told us of this conversation, we hadn't yet known of what lay in store for the ghetto in the coming days. But now, as we heard the calls from the loudspeakers, Grandfather made our decision for us: "We stay in the apartment. Everyone sit on the mattresses; no one go near the windows, so that the soldiers won't discover us."

We stayed seated on the mattresses, and the soldiers raged outside. Grandfather spoke the Yom Kippur prayer for those at home. The "action" lasted throughout the evening. Only then did the soldiers leave the ghetto, taking four thousand men, women, and children with them. They had filled their quota, the required number of Jews to be arrested and taken away that day.

When darkness fell and the holy day was over, Grandfather asked that we all be given tea, bread, and some honey. Yom Kippur had passed, and we ended our fast with a meager meal.

The "actions" lasted fourteen more days, until the end of Sukkoth.* Every day soldiers appeared in the ghetto. With the help of the Jewish police, they broke into apartments, dragged whole families out, and took them away.

Because of this we got used to sitting quietly in the house, and to walking in a crouch, so no one could spot us at the windows. Countless times, soldiers appeared in the courtyard of our building; we often heard them going up and down the stairs. Fear turned us into stones. Motionless and silent, we stayed seated at our places, holding our breath. Even little Fejgele could fall silent in the middle of a word, or freeze in the middle of a step.

We learned to live in expectation and in readiness; it was only luck that no knocks were heard at our door. We had put six weeks in Ghetto 2 behind us, and we were still alive. During that time around sixteen thousand Vilnius Jews were killed.

One day official work permits were distributed. Because they were printed on pink paper, they were called "pink passes." My mother, Julek, Wolodja, and Jechiel had found work, and so the whole family had pink passes.

One's spouse and two children could be included on each pass. Everyone understood that the passes conferred privileges on those who held them and that those privileges had to be shared. The passes were the sole documents; there were no identification papers. Because only names, and no photographs, were on them, it was easy to insert anyone's name. On his pass, for example, Julek named Lena, my mother's sister, as his wife, and Lea and Dolka as his daughters. My mother named my grandfather as her husband, me as her daughter, and the son of an acquaintance as her own. Wolodja and Jechiel also each added an additional child to

* Sukkoth: Harvest festival.

their passes. We had begun to look out for ourselves, and to think ahead about possible difficulties. And because each of us was an only child, the passes also bore the names of the children of neighbors who either hadn't any passes or who had more than two children.

On October 21 the police assembled all those who had passes, along with their families. Loaded down with bundles, we were led through the streets from Ghetto 2. We left through a gate, crossed over Dajtsche Road, and were at last led through a side gate into Ghetto 1, into Rudnicka Street.

Here, in the second house on the right, at Number 2, Rudnicka Street, Wolodja found a big room in a second-story, five-room apartment that still had some space. The other rooms were overcrowded, but in this big room lived only two members of the Jospe family. These two, a brother-in-law and a sister-in-law, had come home from work to find their loved ones gone. The two of them were the only ones left behind after that day's "action" had taken away their entire family.

On a sofa in the big room the two of them sat, frightened and shaken. In the middle of the room stood a big table with chairs around it. Otherwise, it was empty. It looked as if the previous inhabitants had taken everything else with them. We brought in all our belongings and moved into our new lodging. Together with the Jospes, there were fifteen of us in the room, plus the three additional children. Fortunately, after a few days, the children's parents arrived. They had gotten out of Ghetto 2 with the help of our work permit passes. They were happy to find their children healthy and unhurt.

In this move I had had to leave my beloved doll, Bébé, and the doll carriage, behind in Ghetto 2. They hadn't let us take them with us. I was very sad.

Once again we started to settle ourselves into a new residence. In each of the apartment's large rooms, at least ten people were living. Five to eight people lived in the smaller rooms. Like most of the apartments in the neighborhood, the rooms were lined up one after the other, as in a railroad car. Corridors connected them. There were entrances on both sides of the apartment. The main entrance was next to our room. Beside the door was the sole toilet for the entire apartment. All the inhabitants had to go through our room when they wanted to use the toilet. People often stood on line to use the toilet in the long, narrow passage in front of our door.

The kitchen was on the other side of the apartment. It had to be shared among all the families. Each family had its own corner, and its own time to cook. Carrying groceries, the women walked to the kitchen through all the rooms; returning, they carried pots of hot food.

In an apartment crowded with hungry people, there was fussing and quarreling every day. Hunger tormented us all; from time to time, something—a crust of bread, a glass of milk, or a potato—would "disappear." As a result, the mothers quarreled; sometimes, when the men got involved, it even came to blows.

Once again it was Wolodja who succeeded in obtaining boards. Together with Jechiel, he built bunk beds. On the narrow side of the room, he erected three beds. The bottom two were wider; the third, the top one, was somewhat narrower.

On the bottom bunk, Wolodja, Chassia, and Fejgele slept; above them, Julia, Jechiel, and Jochele; and on the top, Lena and Lea. On the longer side of the room he installed a narrower bunk bed. Mama and Julek slept on the bottom, above them Dolka and I. The dining table was left to my grandfather. At night a thin mattress would be laid on top of the table; that was his bed.

The plank platforms served not only as beds; they were really our living room. Even so, you couldn't sit on them properly, because the space between the beds only measured about eighty centimeters (two feet, eight inches). In the lower, broader bunks, you slept as if you were stacked on a shelf.

The foot of each bunk was loaded with bundles and clothes. Any personal conversations, any arguments that took place between a couple on one of the shelves, could be overheard by the ears of those lying close by.

We lived together, on good days and bad days.

We children were not usually allowed to go out into the streets. Sometimes I went walking in the courtyard of the Jewish Council,* but only when it was quiet in the ghetto. The back courtyard of the building at Number 6, Rudnicka Street formed a large, round plaza. The apartments of Gens, the chairman of the Jewish Council, and of Dessler, his deputy, were there. In the middle of the square there was a tree, the only one in the ghetto, because trees and plants had been forbidden to the inhabitants of the ghetto. Around the tree there was a small lawn. A sandy path had been laid out; at its edge stood a few benches. My girlfriends and I went walking there and told each other the news we had heard from the adults.

Judith Kugel, my best and dearest friend, was the same age as I. Our parents had become friends before the war, and I had often visited her with Michla.

We were both intensely interested in what was going on in our surroundings and hungry for the news of the ghetto. We couldn't visit each other, because our living quarters were so cramped, and so we sought out this courtyard,

41

* Jewish Council: Immediately after the incursion of the Germans, a Jewish Council had to be elected in each Jewish district. It was responsible for the exact and expeditious implementation of all German directives. In the ghettos, however, the Jewish Council was never elected, but appointed by the Germans themselves.

where we could meet undisturbed and take a stroll, at least when it was quiet in the ghetto. Sometimes Judith's older cousin, pretty Gita Perlow, accompanied us.

After a time the work passes were changed. The new ones were printed on yellow paper, and so were named "yellow passes." However, the ones for family members now became "blue passes." Each holder of a yellow pass could request blue passes either for his parents or for his spouse and two children, and so everyone made the best use of them. If you didn't have enough children of your own, you would claim others' children. The holders of yellow passes could leave the ghetto to go to work. But blue pass holders could leave only accompanied by the person who had the corresponding yellow pass. There weren't enough jobs in the German factories, so many people stayed in the ghetto without any passes. Many people attempted to link up with pass holders, getting themselves listed as husband, wife, or child. Sometimes they paid bribes. My mother worked in a German sewing shop, Wolodja in a leather shop, and Jechiel in the city gardens, so we had our own passes. Julek was a foreman at the office of public works, which was located next to the municipal buildings.

The next large "action" came to be known as the "action of the yellow passes." On short notice all holders of such passes and their families were taken from the ghetto to their workplaces.

Grandfather went with a group to his workplace, accompanied by Lena as his wife, and by Lea and one of her girlfriends as daughters.

We went to the gate: my mother; a stranger she had named on her pass as her husband; and his son and me, as children. Julek was accompanied by Dolka and a woman with her child.

I went with my mother and the stranger to her workplace. There we sat in a nearby room and waited. The room was for the families of the pass holders who had been summoned there. We children played and didn't pay much attention to the overall tension.

In the evening the groups returned to the ghetto. My mother was very nervous, because she didn't know what had happened in the ghetto that day. We also hadn't heard anything from Julek and Dolka; they had gone to Julek's workplace.

The ghetto appeared dead. Five thousand people with no yellow passes were taken away that day. Lithuanian policemen had taken them from their hiding places and deported them.

We went through the gates and ran to our apartment. Julek and Dolka had returned ahead of us, and had been afraid something had happened to us.

A week later, on October 29, 1941, we learned of the liquidation of Ghetto 2. Then, on November 3, another "action" took place that went down in the annals of the ghetto as the "second action of the yellow passes."

Even though both Julek and my mother possessed yellow passes, this time my mother refused to go without Julek. She didn't want to be separated from him again, and she was afraid to go through the gates on her own. Besides that, Julek's workplace was in an office of the municipal building; my mother's, on the other hand, was in the sewing shop. They had already told us that families would stay three days at the workplaces. So my mother relinquished her pass (with its accompanying blue passes for a husband and two children) to a woman friend of hers; we left the ghetto on Julek's pass.

While we were waiting at the gate, Gita Perlow was standing on line in front of us with her grandparents. She was a strikingly pretty girl with tanned skin, big brown eyes, thick hair, and a beautiful figure. She looked like a movie star. Because only Gita worked, the Perlows possessed only one yellow pass and the two blue ones belonging to her parents. But Gita had decided to rescue her entire family on her pass. Therefore, early that morning, she had left the ghetto with her parents and had taken them to her workplace. Then she had taken the yellow star off her clothing and had run back to the ghetto through side streets. She made it, as a matter of fact, and got back in through a side door. Now, two hours after her first trip, the yellow star back on her chest, she was again standing at the main gate, along with her grandparents, who she said were her parents.

But Franz Murer, the boss of the ghetto,* was standing at the gate. He remembered the pretty young girl who had caught his eye as she went by with her parents earlier that morning. He stopped the groups. We were waiting in line behind Gita. We didn't know she had already gone through the gate once; we wondered why Murer was stopping her. We saw the Germans checking the young girl; and suddenly all three, the grandparents and the grandchild, were led from the gate into a side street.

Now it was our turn in line. We were nervous and anxious, because it was always dangerous to pass the sentries at the gate. The German officer looked at us and checked our papers. Suddenly a series of gunshots rang out. No one reacted to the gunshots. We were passed, and we went on. And there, in the side street off the gate, lay three bodies: the old grandparents, and next to them their pretty granddaughter, Gita. They lay just at the edge of the street, and their blood ran over the sidewalk. My mother turned my head in the other direction, but still, I had seen them. I saw Murer and his troops go back to the ghetto gates. Their steps rang on the pavement. Murer looked gratified. He had the

44

* From September 1941 through 1943, Franz Murer was Deputy District Commissar. Hans Hingst was the District Commissar.

right to use any suppressive measures necessary against those who were "not truthful." No one who lied to a German officer escaped unpunished.

Murer's name alone roused fear and terror in the ghetto. Not one of us dared go outside when we heard Murer was in the ghetto. Horrors were told of this man; he had been responsible for the murders of many of Vilnius' Jews.

Time and again the people who were working outside the ghetto tried to smuggle food in. The skimpy rations we received at the hands of the Jewish Council were not enough to live on. Franz Murer usually came to the ghetto gates when the work crews were returning. He drove his auto into the crowd and pointed at someone at random. The poor wretch was checked by the policemen to see if he had perhaps tried to smuggle something to eat into the ghetto under his clothes. If something was actually found—a kilo of semolina or sugar—the person caught was taken to prison, to Lukiszki. But before that he was severely beaten while still at the gates.

When Murer stood at the gates, you tried to warn the returnees that they shouldn't, for God's sake, bring anything in with them; then they got rid of their smuggled goods. If a woman was stopped, she had to undress, and Murer ordered her and her clothes to be searched. She would be cruelly beaten as a punishment even for half a loaf of bread.

Winters were hard in Vilnius, and it was now especially cold. We had no heating fuel and sat in the cold apartments, in bed, fully dressed, and covered by the thin blankets that had been made available to us. We children forgot to play; we forgot to laugh; we were sad and frozen, always hungry. We learned to live quietly and keep our eyes open, and to eavesdrop on the conversations of the adults. From these conversations we came to learn everything that took place in the ghetto. The adults had long ago stopped trying to conceal anything from us; they had stopped speaking Russian among themselves so that we wouldn't understand.

From time to time our dear, loyal Mania would come to the ghetto gates. She'd ask those who entered to send us her regards and let us know she was in town and would come around to the main gates at certain times. In this manner she succeeded in seeing my mother every few months, and in bringing us something to eat: bread, cheese, sometimes even meat—true delicacies compared to our poor nourishment.

I often saw an old man sitting on the steps of our house. His clothes were dirty and torn; he had a wild, gray beard, and he clutched a broken tin plate beneath his padded coat. I heard the adults talking about him; they were discussing what they should do about him.

I was sorry for him, and one day I gave him my shawl. I was very surprised that my mother wasn't angry with me for having done that. I asked her who the man who lived in our stairwell was. I learned that he was an uncle of my mother's—an older brother of my dead grandmother—Great-Uncle Miron.

He was a well-bred man and had lived alone his whole life. He had taught school and had occupied himself with philosophy. A pleasant and quiet person. When the war started, he found himself with no means, no students, and no home.

Nor did he find any refuge in the ghetto. Having once accidentally met Grandfather, he had followed him home and hunkered down on our steps. We couldn't take him in with us; there was no more room. Uncle Miron was not working, and so he got no food from the Jewish Council. He had sunk further and further; now, on our steps, he was completely addled.

My mother liked him very much and took the trouble

to make sure he got one warm meal a day; that was all she could do for him. All that spring our old uncle stayed in our stairwell. When the "old people's action" took place, he disappeared, and we never saw him again.

The "old people's action," which took place on July 26, 1942, etched itself into my memory. My grandfather had a sister who had been widowed while still young; she had remained alone with her three children, Grischa, Dora, and Genia. My grandfather had supported and cared for his younger sister and her children his whole life. My mother's cousins and our family were very close; they had always spent holidays and special days at Grandfather's.

We met them again here, in Ghetto 1.

My great-aunt's oldest son, Grischa, had been a Communist before the war. In the mid-thirties, when the campaigns against the Communists reached their peak in Poland, he had succeeded in getting over the border to the Soviet Union. There, a bitter surprise awaited him. He was arrested, accused of being a Trotskyite,* and sent to Siberia, where he vanished without a trace.

During the Russian occupation of Vilnius his sister Dora had married her friend Mulja Pariser. He was also a Communist, and he worked at Elektrit, a precision instrument and radio apparatus company. The Soviet authorities transported the company to the Soviet Union, and the whole workforce, including Mulja Pariser and his young wife, ended up in Minsk. Their son, Lonja, was born there.

Destiny is an odd thing. One day a woman came to the door of the small apartment in Minsk in which the Parisers lived. She was Grischa's wife. To her great joy, Dora now

* Trotskyite: Strictly speaking, a follower of the political teachings of Leon Trotsky; in the Soviet Union, however, also used to designate all leftist critics of the system.

learned that her brother was alive. His Siberian prison sentence would be over in two more years. The wife had brought their daughter, Natasha, with her. She had been born in Siberia and was a very pretty girl, with exotic features and dark hair—a real Siberian.

At once they requested, and obtained, travel permits for Dora; Dora's son, Lonja; and Natasha. They came to Vilnius to spend the summer with Dora's mother, my great-aunt. Two days after their arrival, the war had broken out.

My great-aunt, Genia, Dora, Lonja, and Natasha were living in the ghetto in a basement room not far from us. On the day of the "old people's action," Genia came to us in extreme need. The Jewish police had arrested her mother and taken her to a truck that stood beside the main gates. We thought we had gotten used to the disappearance of so many people from the ghetto. When it was someone we knew, however, or a family member, it was a heavy blow. Our sadness was great; I hid up in the top bunk, as I always did when I wanted to be alone with my feelings.

Grandfather wanted to go out and look for help for his sister. But it was clear that an "action" was taking place whose target was old people, and so everyone decided to hide him. He climbed into a clothes closet in the hallway, and my mother closed the door after him and locked it with a key.

Julek left the apartment. He wanted to attempt to rescue the aunt. The rest of us waited.

Suddenly we heard running steps and cries in the courtyard. The apartment door was thrown open, and a small, nimble old woman stumbled in. She ran blindly into our room and hid behind the door. Jewish and Lithuanian policemen ran in behind her, shouting and striking out at all sides with their clubs. The terrified old woman came out of her hiding place and ran about the room, looking for an exit. A Lithuanian policeman ran after her, his club in his raised hand. He went directly by my bunk, so that I could see the murderous expression on his face. I felt his heavy breath and smelled the odor of vodka. Like a mad animal, he pursued his quarry. The woman ran from room to room, through the whole apartment. I pulled the blanket over my head and saw nothing more. I only heard the policemen running. One of them shouted in Yiddish at us, "Murderers! Hand over the old people, or they'll kill us all!" Then they caught the poor old woman and dragged her away through the back door.

When the "action" was over, Julek returned with the aunt. Outside near the truck he had searched for someone with whom he could plead for her rescue. Finally he succeeded in bribing a Jewish policeman, who pushed the old woman from the tailgate just as the truck began to drive away.

When he came back to our apartment, Julek was pale with shock and his words stuck in his throat. He had witnessed pitiful old people being loaded into trucks—people who didn't understand what was happening to them. They tried to flee; they were captured and brutally beaten, and were finally driven away. Julek had also heard Gens speaking on the street, outside. He had heard Gens commanding people to give up their old people, so that the young ones could survive.

Gens, the head of the Jewish Council, and his deputy, Dessler, carried out the commands of Officer Franz Murer, the German ghetto boss. The strategy of Gens and Dessler was: "Give the Germans the victims they demand; choose the old and the sick to sacrifice, in order to save some of the people, especially the young and the strong."

Not everyone in the ghetto agreed with this decision; most people cared for their parents and were not ready to sacrifice them in order to save themselves. The different political organizations in the ghetto, especially, fought against this strategy of the Jewish Council.

At the start of the war between Germany and the Soviet Union, over sixty thousand Jews had lived in Vilnius. One year after we had been sent to the ghetto, after all the "actions" we had survived, we still numbered about eighteen thousand Jews.

On quiet days my mother allowed me to go out and visit Grandfather Weksler. Before the war he had lived in a big apartment in Zawalna Street, not far from Fortuna, his candy and chocolate factory.

Grandfather Weksler was an imposing man, big and broad-shouldered, with short blond hair and a reddish mustache whose ends curled up, in the style of Emperor Franz Joseph. He had a good, merry face. He always wore a top hat and carried a walking stick in his hand, which he swung back and forth as he walked. He made public appearances, gave speeches at the association of Jewish industrialists in Vilnius, and was a member of the association's board of directors.

Grandfather Weksler had two sons and two daughters, as well as a stepdaughter his second wife had brought with her to the marriage. Grandfather's oldest daughter, Mina, had emigrated to Palestine in the thirties. Grandfather was a Zionist and encouraged his children to emigrate to Eretz Israel. He bought land there, and he hoped he could spend his final years in the Holy Land and die there.

Two years after his daughter Mina was born, my father, Isak, was born. His mother died in childbirth, and Grandfather was left alone with two small children. As was then the custom, he took into his house a woman who had just lost her own child, and who could nurse his newborn. Isak loved his nurse and thrived, and she loved the boy like a mother.

My grandfather took a shine to the woman. He married her and adopted Ljuba, her daughter from her first marriage, as his own. Ljuba was fat and ugly, and it was difficult to find a husband for her. Grandfather took the trouble to find a quiet young man who took her as his wife for a large dowry settlement. The couple had two daughters: Elke, who was my age; and Hella, who was four years younger. After a few years of unhappy marriage, Ljuba's husband left her, and she stayed at Grandfather's house with her two daughters.

Elke was not a pretty child either. She was clumsy and had a big nose, but she was a good, quiet girl. Everyone pitied her and was very patient with her. She was dear to me, and because we were the same age, she became my playmate. I liked to go to Grandfather Weksler's and play with Elke.

Tanja, Grandfather Weksler's third child, was a very pretty woman with laughing green eyes. She was merry, liked to sing, and was always the center of attention. Tanja was very devoted to Mina, her older sister; when she got the opportunity in 1938, she traveled to Eretz Israel to be with her.

Schneior, the youngest child of the family, was a well-built man with a long, pale face and thick, dark-blond hair. He loved sports and participated in the riding competitions and swimming races held by the Maccabee Athletic Club. Schneior was a very jolly man, always in the mood for a joke. He always lifted me up high, and liked to set me on top of any closet in the room. I was very proud of my tall, slim uncle.

Schneior greatly loved his older brother, my father, and was always asking him for advice. He married Schejndl, a good-looking young woman who had come to Vilnius from one of the outlying shtetls;* the two had a little daughter, Sarele.

Grandfather Weksler was a good-hearted man, and cared for the people who worked for him. Most of them were Jews, and Grandfather Weksler took an interest in their lives and knew their personal difficulties. When one of them had a daughter who was getting married, Grandfather Weksler would add something to the dowry, and he would keep a lookout for an apartment for the young couple. If one of his workers had a son born, Grandfather arranged the bris, or ritual circumcision, and, later on, the bar mitzvah.** If one of his female workers was widowed, he helped her feed her family, and took an interest in the children. The workers loved their boss, respected him greatly, and saw themselves as part of a large family.

Grandfather Weksler, who was loved by all who knew him, was well-to-do but didn't amass a fortune. He kept a big house, his sons and daughters were raised well and lacked for nothing, but their manner of living was modest. They wore no jewelry, and there were few valuables and no gold coins in their house. My grandfather wasn't sparing when he could help others, and he freely gave money for worthy causes. He always prayed in Vilnius' big synagogue, the Chorshul, and was considered one of its most noteworthy members.

He himself worked in the candy factory, preparing the hot sugar mixtures from which the candy was made. I always wondered about his ability to sample the sugars. He didn't care for sweets himself, but he always made special, uniquely shaped candies for us, his grandchildren.

In the ghetto Grandfather and Grandmother Weksler

---

* Shtetl (Yiddish): Pre-World War II term for an eastern European locality settled predominantly by Jews.

** Bar mitzvah: Religious coming-of-age rite for Jewish males who have reached the age of thirteen.

lived in a room that had once been part of a store. Ljuba and her daughters also lived with them. Schneior, Schejndl, and Sarele lived in the same house, on the floor above them. Only Schneior had work, as a mechanic in the German car factory. Because they had only one yellow pass, the Wekslers suffered hunger and cold. With luck, they had succeeded in surviving the many "actions"; most of the time they sat at home, sad and depressed.

Grandfather Weksler became ill and my mother began to send me to him often, carrying food—a hot soup, or potatoes. Grandmother was always glad when I came; she kissed me and cried. She loved my father; after all, she had raised him, and she longed for him. My grandfather had aged years since he had learned my father had been arrested by the Germans and, presumably, killed in Ponary. I often saw him crying and taking sedatives for his heart condition.

One day Schneior came and told us that Grandfather had died of heart failure. We all went to his apartment and accompanied the dead man to the gates of the ghetto. This was how bodies were disposed of in the ghetto, since it was forbidden for Jews to go to the cemetery outside the ghetto. No member of the family learned where Grandfather Weksler was buried. Then we went back and sat shiva* in our grandparents' small room. Grandfather Indurski said, "Aba Weksler was a righteous man and died a peaceful death in his own bed. He was spared great sorrow. Who among us can say how we will die, and what we must endure before our time is come?" At that time none of us had any hint yet just how right his words were.

I had recently noticed that Chassia wasn't feeling well in the mornings. It was hard for her to get up, and she often vomited.

53

---

* Shiva: The strict seven-day period of mourning following the death of a family member, during which the family sits together and mourns.

I didn't understand the reason and thought that she had eaten some spoiled food. But the vomiting didn't stop.

Chassia and Wolodja were the youngest couple in the family. They had married in 1936. Wolodja was my mother's younger brother, and after finishing high school, he had begun to work in his father's glove factory. For Grandfather

WOLODJA AND CHASSIA
1938

Indurski it was a great disappointment. He had dreamed his only son would study at the university, and had therefore obtained admission for him, although by that time, there was a quota for Jewish students. But Wolodja didn't want to study.

He was a happy young man, good-looking and athletic. He had been a member of the Maccabee Sports Club and had pursued all kinds of sports: ice-skating, swimming, kayaking. He had also got to know his future wife, Chassia, at the Maccabee. She was a very beautiful girl, as happy and athletic as he. She was brown-skinned, with thick brown hair, big, black, shining eyes, and a snub nose.

A year after the marriage, a son had been born to them, but he died in infancy. The young mother was sad and depressed. After complicated medical treatments, Chassia bore a daughter. The baby was born two months after Grandmother's death, and so she received her name—Fejgele. When we went to the ghetto, Fejgele was just three years old. Now, in the cramped quarters of a single room, and despite the harsh ban on conception for Jewish women, Chassia was pregnant again.

Pregnant women had to contend with the most severe penalties; therefore, everyone tried to keep Chassia's pregnancy a secret and to find a way to end it. Chassia wanted the child, and cried her eyes out. She finally came to see she would have to end the pregnancy. There was no possibility of going to a doctor. The ghetto doctors had neither offices nor the instruments necessary to perform an abortion. And so the women of the family looked for another way to help Chassia.

Very rarely could you get a pass to go to the bathhouse, which was in Ghetto 2. In our ghetto there was no public bathhouse. You merely washed yourself in your apartment at a basin of cold water, and in an overcrowded room at that. So I was glad when my mother decided to get a bathing pass for me, Dolka, Chassia, and herself.

One Sunday morning we joined a group of women and made our way to the bathhouse. My mother immediately opted for the single baths. Most women washed themselves in the big public room, but this time my mother paid a great deal of money for three single cubicles: one for Chassia, one for Dolka, and one for herself and me. We had a half hour to get washed.

My mother was nervous and didn't take much care in washing me. She hurried, herself, and immediately got dressed. And she was listening all the time to hear what was happening next door, in Chassia's cubicle.

Suddenly we heard a scream, and my mother ran next door. Chassia had lost consciousness there, in a hot tub filled with blood. With the help of other women, my mother succeeded in reviving Chassia, washing, and drying her.

We went back to Ghetto 1, my mother and Dolka propping Chassia up the whole way. Wolodja was waiting for us at home. He was pale, and when he saw us, he didn't relax; he hugged his wife and cried.

Only much later did I understand that a woman who worked in the bathhouse had assisted Chassia by performing an abortion.

In June 1942 a new German monster appeared, in the form of Martin Weiss. He had replaced Franz Murer. He drove through the streets of the ghetto acting like an absolute ruler. Time and again he would praise people's work, but afterward one of his attendants would order the workers concerned arrested and taken to Ponary. Therefore, he was also known by the name "Weiss, the Black,"* the executioner of Ponary.

---

* Translator's note: There is a paradoxical pun in this nickname. In German "weiss" means "white"; therefore, Martin Weiss's nickname was "White, the Black."

In the autumn of 1942 a few houses in a neighboring street were incorporated into the ghetto. Julek succeeded in garnering a small room in the new section, and we four moved to it. The family members remaining behind also had an easier time of it, then; there were now only eleven of them in the room.

Our new place was the middle room of a three-room apartment. We took our bunk bed there, too. It didn't bother us that the ceiling was lower there, because now we could sit at a table and not have to always live in bed.

There was a small table in the room, along with a double-door clothes closet. Now we could hang up our clothes and didn't need to keep them under the mattress in the bed. There was also an iron stove. My mother cooked our food and our tea on it, so the room was kept warm, too.

On our right lived the Levins: a rabbi, his wife, and his mother. They were very religious people. Both women wore headscarves. They had to go though our room whenever they went to the toilet or the kitchen, or when they wanted to leave the house. Rabbi Levin's mother was old and clumsy. She usually sat in their room preparing the family's poor meals on a small alcohol stove.

The rabbi's wife was mentally ill and never left the room. Although we lived together almost a whole year, I was only to see her once or twice. She was short, thin, and inadequately dressed in a sort of brown nightgown. Her hair was uncombed, and her eyes had a crazy look. She often had raging fits; then she would scream, beat on the wall with her fists, and blame her husband for everything bad that was happening. He tried to calm her with quiet words. When the fits lasted too long, he had to give her strong medicine, and she then fell into a daze and went to sleep. In the mornings when he came out of their room with the chamber pot, a nauseating smell permeated the room. Poor, quiet Rabbi Levin had a hard life. He was torn between worries about food and medicine for his wife, and Torah studies. My mother often conversed with him. He was an intelligent, cultivated man.

The room on the left was bigger. In it lived a family with two children. We and our neighbors had to go through this room in order to go to the toilet or fetch water. It wasn't pleasant for any of us, but we soon got used to this state of affairs.

Secretly, a school was established in the ghetto, and my mother sent me to it. I was in the third grade. Lessons were held in Yiddish. I loved school and was learning eagerly. A great deal of our learning was memorization, since we had neither sufficient notebooks nor textbooks. When SS men or Lithuanian policemen were close by, we immediately began to sing or play, so they wouldn't discover that learning was going on in the ghetto.

Almost all the children in school suffered from painful, festering sores, brought on by a lack of nutrition and vitamins. I had sores too, mostly around my mouth. My lips hurt, and I couldn't eat solid food. About this time, first-aid stations were established in the ghetto. True, there was no medicine there, but we children with sores received a daily drink made from yeast steeped in hot water. It was a disgusting mixture with a sharp smell. But because I was always hungry, I soon got used to this medicine. Every day, on the way home from school, I went to the station and drank a glass of the light-brown liquid.

It wasn't long before another "action" took place. One day when I came home from school, the big room in our apartment was empty. The family with the two children had been taken away.

Were we getting inured to having people in our surroundings disappear? Were our feelings dulled? Were our hearts becoming hard, and were we losing all feeling? I began to think about it—about what was going on around me, seeing it all through my ten-year-old eyes. In school our teachers told us as much as possible about the past. We learned Jewish history. We came to know about the roots of the people of Israel, about the heroes there had once been. I asked myself where they were now. In this time of want, we had need of heroes: people who would help us and rescue us. But there were none to be found.

I began to dream of a brighter future, and to write small poems.

The Time Is Not Far

There will come a time,
and the time is not far,
when from east and from west,
from every side,
light will arrive,
and a warm wind,
and the clouds will
all disappear quickly.
Oh, believe me, my friend,
the time is not far!

A children's choir was started in the ghetto, and I joined it. We had many rehearsals; two or three times we appeared before the public in a hall. We sang under the leadership of Opeskin, the teacher, and were directed in performance by the famous conductor Slep.

The food situation in the ghetto got steadily worse. My mother tried to get in touch with Olga and Vera, the women to whom she had entrusted many of our things before our removal to the ghetto. Now she wanted to get some of the things back, in order to trade them for something to eat: for bread and potatoes. But when she informed them of a meeting through a Polish message boy, neither Olga nor Vera showed up at the appointed hour. Our need and hunger had become so great that my mother risked her life and went to the Polish women herself.

Vera wouldn't let my mother into her apartment at all. Through her closed door she yelled at my mother to go away, or she would call the German police.

My mother fled from there and went to Olga's apartment. Before the war my mother had greatly helped Olga's family in a financial emergency. She had also assisted at her wedding. With her own hands she had helped set up the apartment in which she was still living. Olga led my mother into the kitchen and gave her tea and a piece of bread. But when my mother asked for some of her things back, Olga lied and said she had never gotten anything from my mother. She began shouting and chased my mother from the house.

From time to time we got some groceries from Mania, our former housekeeper. But the streets of Vilnius and its environs had also become dangerous for a Polish woman. Mania came every couple of months, bringing something to eat, and inquiring after me. She could meet only in secret with my mother, usually near my mother's workplace. Mania suggested to my mother that I be given to her. She would take me back to the village with her; there I would have everything I needed. But my mother wavered.

One evening, after one of Mania's visits, we sat down to eat, and there was bread, butter, quark,* and jam. These were delicacies with which we were very sparing. That evening I took a slice of bread, spread butter on it, and also put some jam on top. I bit into it and licked my lips with satisfaction. Dolka wanted jam on her buttered bread, too,

---

* Translator's note: "Quark" is a middle and eastern European food that is something like yogurt, something like cottage cheese, but not precisely either. It is usually sweet.

but Julek wouldn't let her have any. "You can eat bread with butter or bread with jam. We have to be sparing with these delicacies," he said.

Dolka cried and didn't want to give in. She pointed at me and complained that I could do anything I wanted. Julek tried to stick up for me. He said I was still little and needed to grow; that I was a poor, fatherless child. But Dolka would have none of his justifications; she started screaming and it ended in a big fight.

The upshot of all this was that I felt I had won. I was happy that Julek had taken my side. But that night in bed, when Dolka turned away from me, I was sorry about my behavior. I cried quietly and begged for her forgiveness.

The next morning I hid the piece of bread I received. When we left the house, I gave it to Dolka. Dolka, who was always hungry, took it, but then she gave half of it back to me. We hugged and kissed each other; we were friends once again. This understanding and our friendship lasted for the rest of the time we had together.

The big room in our apartment didn't remain empty long. New inhabitants arrived: a very large family, parents with many grown sons and daughters. After the closing of many smaller ghettos near the city, this family had been sent to the Vilnius ghetto.

They were a Jewish farm family from one of the outlying villages. They were friendly and cheerful. In the evenings they often sang and played every game imaginable. They also laughed a lot. These people hadn't yet known hunger or cold. They arrived directly from their village, and their good humor and optimism had an effect on us, too. We became calmer.

The mood didn't last long. When it was announced that all people from the villages had to assemble with their luggage in the courtyard, to be sent to Germany to work in the fields, our neighbors decided to go along. My mother, who

61

no longer believed the rumors of work camps, pleaded with them not to leave the apartment. We had already learned from our experiences; we knew there were specific quotas the police must fill for each "action." When it was filled, the "action" would also end. So we knew it was worthwhile to hide, hoping not to be discovered while the "action" was still going on.

But our neighbors were naive. They had been sitting idly in the apartment, and they had neither work nor a pass. They hoped they would get larger food rations in a work camp, and their lives would be more secure. And so they took their leave of us, cheerfully, hoping we would all meet, healthy and well, after the war.

During this "action" five thousand people were murdered in Ponary. All the Jews from the villages were killed on the same day. With their deaths, the Jewish settlements—the villages and shtetls—were obliterated. We found this out from a survivor, who had only been wounded in the mass shooting, and who had managed to crawl out of the grave, and make his way back to the ghetto.

THE
MALINA

A TEMPORARY QUIET settled over the ghetto. Despite that, many of the inhabitants decided to look for hiding places for themselves and their families.

There were not many options. A few families sought shelter outside the ghetto, on the Aryan side, in the Polish neighborhoods. Some looked for refuge with acquaintances or former neighbors, as well as other "good" people who allowed themselves to be paid dearly for the "goodness of their hearts." Those rich people who had managed to hold on to their assets could afford temporary hiding places outside the ghetto. But even these weren't secure. Yet after everything they endured in the ghetto, after all the rumors that had reached us about the fate of Jews outside, many Jews held on to their money and possessions and hoped that nothing would happen to them.

Resistance organizations had formed in the ghetto. Their membership was predominantly young people. My older cousin, Lea, was in contact with the ghetto's Fighting Youth. Now she offered us their help. She wanted to take us into the forests, to the partisans. That way we too could make our contribution to the fight against the Nazis.

The negotiations with the resistance and the partisans were slow and laborious. Lea could have joined them at once, but for groups as large as ours, it took much time to reach an agreement with the partisans. Finally, they told us we should ready ourselves. We would have to leave the ghetto through the sewer system. Then we would make our way along many different contact points on the outside, in order to reach the partisans in the forests.

On the agreed-upon day we were ready and dressed for the dangerous undertaking. Then it suddenly came out that not all of us were wanted in the woods. The partisans were ready only to take the healthy and the strong. They didn't want to take Lea's mother, Lena, a delicate woman who had recently been ill often. They maintained that a woman as weak as she would endanger the whole group on the long and difficult route to the forests. And my seventy-year-old grandfather was too old. Even though he was sound as a bell, the partisans refused to take him. Neither would they take me, a ten-year-old, to say nothing of seven-year-old Jochele and four-year-old Fejgele.

At that time we still believed we'd all remain together; the thought of a separation hadn't crossed our minds. Lea refused to leave the ghetto without her mother, and under no circumstances would my mother go without me. So we all stayed together in the ghetto and began to look around for another way out. Jechiel got in touch with a farm family in Puszkarnia, the farm that he had had earlier. Now he was hoping to find shelter and work with them for himself and his wife.

Julek and my mother decided to look for a hiding place within the ghetto. Julek was the foreman of a Jewish work squad that carried out maintenance work in the Aryan section of the city. Since he was tall and had light-brown hair and an Aryan-looking face, he could be taken for a typical German. Besides that, he spoke perfect German. He had been born in the Polish province of Galicia, studied at a German school, and served time in the Austrian army. The Germans actually saw him as almost one of their own. They gave him a responsible post and relied on him. He had to assemble work crews according to their skills and send them to assigned places in the city where they made repairs and did cleaning and construction work. The work crews were composed of construction workers, carpenters, glaziers, plumbers, and—most important—sewer cleaners and chimney sweeps.

Over time tight groups had formed to work outside the ghetto. These had established contact with the Polish population. Through them, food was smuggled into the ghetto— over the roofs and through the sewer pipes. Through them, people were smuggled out of the ghetto. By the same means, weapons were smuggled in for the underground organizations.

Julek shut his eyes to these activities, although he took no direct hand in them. When it was necessary to arrange a secret operation, he invented some work so a work crew could be sent to a specific part of the city.

Once, a chimney sweep was arrested, a member of the Feintuch family. He was delivered up to Julek's immediate superior, an SS man responsible for the smooth functioning of labor crews in the department of public works at City Hall. This SS man was a senior officer, cultivated, but decidedly brutal. The arrested man therefore stood in great danger. His family came to see us. They sat for a long time in our room, discussing with Julek how they might rescue the man, while my mother, Dolka, and I were with our neighbors in the next room. I don't know what they decided to do, but next day, before he went to work, Julek embraced my mother for a long time, and she warned him again and again to be especially careful.

It was a very long day.

My mother was horribly nervous. In the course of that day several people came by whom I had never seen before. They brought something to eat, sat together with us, and conversed quietly with one another. We waited.

Julek came home very late. It was dark outside, and curfew had already begun when he arrived, staggering and red-faced. Very loudly, he said, "Everything's all right! Tomorrow, he'll come back after work." Then he fell down on the bed and fell asleep at once, still in his clothes.

It grew quiet in the room. Everybody saw that Julek was dead drunk, and he wasn't a drinking man. It was clear he had had a hard and dangerous day trying to rescue the man. But no one knew for sure if he had really succeeded. One after another, our visitors left the room.

Next day, when the work crews came back to the ghetto, the relatives of the arrested man stood near the gates and waited. And suddenly they saw him in a group of chimney sweeps.

This had all happened a few days before Purim.* On the eve of Purim our room was filled with *shalach monoth*, traditional festival presents. Anonymously and in secret, all the ghetto chimney-sweep families sent us packages with food. In them were delicacies we hadn't seen in a long time. My attention was riveted by a whole basket of eggs. I hadn't seen an egg for a long time; I had even forgotten what eggs looked like. My mother forbade me to touch them, so they wouldn't get broken. I hadn't known they were so breakable.

I also saw "hamantaschen" again, the special cookies eaten at Purim. These were large and soft and filled with jam. My mother gave one each to me and to Dolka; the rest she hid under the bed. That evening we closed the doors to our room and sat down to a holiday meal. But the neighbors in the two other rooms smelled the aroma of food. They opened the doors a crack and peered in. With a heavy heart, my mother took some of the food and shared it with the neighbors.

It was a very happy Purim holiday for us.

The next day my mother took the rest of the haman-

66

---

* Purim: A joyous festival on the anniversary of the deliverance of the Jews in ancient Persia.

taschen, packed them up well so no one on the street could see them, and took them to Grandfather and the rest of the family. There was great joy. Everyone ate, and Grandfather drank a shot of the vodka he saved for special occasions. The two Jospes were still sharing the room; when they came home from work, they too got a hamantasch, which they divided.

Mania got in touch with us once again. She had heard of the recent extermination of the village Jews, and had decided to take me home with her. In the previous months she had already visited the city a few times, and had met with my mother at her workplace. She promised to look after me well, and to take care of me. She proposed passing me off in the village as her illegitimate daughter. This good woman was ready to weather the scandal of being an unwed mother in order to rescue me. But when she came with a horse-drawn wagon to take me with her, my mother couldn't find the strength to part with me, and Mania returned to her village as alone as she had come.

Because Julek and my mother had found no hiding place, they turned to the head of the Feintuch family for advice. Mr. Feintuch came to our house. He was a tall, broad-shouldered man, with a round face and round, brown eyes. I loved him immediately. I went to him, took his warm hand in mine and stroked it. As long as he was with us, I didn't budge from his side. I was surprised that a chimney sweep could be so clean and white. In their discussion they reached an agreement that Julek would share in the financing of a big hiding place that some families wanted to build. Moreover, he would help in obtaining the necessary building materials. The four of us could then use the hiding place, the malina,* when it became necessary. The malina

* Malina: In the argot of the underworld, a hiding place for criminals and stolen goods.

would be available only for the use of those who shared in building it. Money alone couldn't buy a place in it. Besides us there were masons, plumbers, electricians, an engineer, a doctor, sewer cleaners, and four chimney-sweep families who would share it.

Building the malina took months. During the whole time, we lived in fear. When the malina was finally finished, there began to be telltale signs that a big "action" was coming.

One day someone from the malina committee let us know we'd have to be in the courtyard of the house across the street in a few hours, to go down to the hiding place.

The courtyard was very large, hemmed in by five-story houses on all sides; an empty square between dirty gray walls, crumbling plaster, and many windows, most of which were glued shut with dark or black paper. Almost all the windowpanes were broken or had cracks. They looked like open wounds, like blind eyes. Where the walls of the houses met the pavement, there were windows that looked as if the ground had swallowed half of them. When it rained, water and slime from the courtyard flowed through these small windows. They were cellar windows, and people lived behind them, too. Hundreds of people lived about this courtyard. In the archways that led from one house into the next courtyard, there were painted doorways on the right and left, fastened with padlocks. These were the houses' latrines. Most of the apartments in the ghetto didn't have toilets; they had communal latrines. There were four to each courtyard, and the inhabitants had a key. There were often fights about the communal latrines.

The malina had been built beneath one of two side-by-side latrines. Hidden water faucets had been installed beneath one of the toilet bowls. When they were turned, the drainage from the second bowl could be blocked. This would keep waste from getting into the part of the pipes that drained from the second toilet.

After the flow was blocked, a pump had to be worked for four hours to siphon off waste from the closed part of the pipe to the open part. After the pumping, the toilet was flushed a few more times. If you then took out the screws at the front of the toilet bowl, you could raise the bowl and tip it back onto the floor. Underneath, in the now-clear sewer pipe, there was a double iron folding trapdoor. If you now slid a pole through the iron rings attached to the two doors, and pulled with all your might at it, you could lift the doors and unfold both sides of the opening.

Under the folding door a hole about four meters (thirteen feet) deep had been dug into the foundations of the building. Into one side of this hole had been set a heavy iron door, like the door to a safe. Behind it two spacious rooms had been built: the first somewhat smaller, the second, as large as a hall. In one corner of the hall there was an outlet connected to the chimney of the building, which reached all the way to the roof. The shaft was furnished with an iron ladder, and was so narrow that only the "Małpes," the "monkeys," could get through it. They were members of one of the chimney-sweep families; I knew them only by their nickname. This tiny shaft served as ventilation; it provided the only air supply for the whole hiding place. The members of the committee who had planned and built the hiding place had installed a water pipe and faucet for fresh-water needs, as well as a pipe connected to the sewer that served as a toilet. They had also provided electricity; from the ceiling hung two lightbulbs. They had built double-decker wood bunks and set up essential equipment. There were blankets and pillows for each bed, and in the first room there were nonperishable food supplies and preserves that would last the inhabitants of the malina for a week. First aid had also been provided, especially sedatives.

Our malina had room for only a certain number of people. When the big "action" began, and the inhabitants of the malina gathered in the courtyard in front of the entrance to the latrine, its existence became known to the other inhabitants of the building. They too tried to push their way inside. It was hard for those in charge to turn people down. Moreover, most families were bringing along a sister, a brother, or another family member with them at the last minute. More people were trying to push into the hiding place than had been anticipated; actual fights broke out at the entrance. This was dangerous; we didn't wish to attract the attention of the Germans or Jewish policemen roaming the ghetto, under any circumstances.

My mother, Julek, Dolka, and I had arrived early. Members of the committee noticed us among all the waiting people. They made a path and conducted us to the entrance of the latrine. Julek decided my mother should climb in first. I saw her shrink back from the dirty hole that gaped before her, but then she climbed down into the stinking pit. I was next in line. The darkness and the stifling air frightened me. They buckled a belt about me. Cables were attached on both sides. Two men held these cables. I wanted to scream; the stink was unendurable. I was sickened and fearful. But before I knew what was happening, Mr. Feintuch was at my side. He put one warm hand over my mouth. With his other, the index finger at his lips, he signaled me to be quiet. Quickly, the men hoisted me over the hole of the pit and let me down on the cables, four meters (thirteen feet) into the depths. When my feet touched the wet, slippery earth, my mother hugged me and immediately pushed me through the iron door into the first room of the malina. Many people were already standing about. Someone said we ought to go on into the second room and take our places on the assigned beds.

My mother remained in the front part a bit longer, until Dolka and, after her, Julek had been let down. Then we went into the hall and looked for the two beds reserved for us. It turned out that strangers had managed to get in before us. They had already claimed one of our beds. Only a wide upper bed remained for the four of us. Julek and my mother felt they could do nothing about the lack of space. Dolka and I climbed up onto the bed. More and more people filled the hall, until the last place was taken. People stood in the corridors; about twenty were still waiting outside, in the smaller room.

Those who had helped the others down now climbed down themselves. The last one closed and locked the toilet door with a key, tipped the toilet bowl back down into place, and bolted the double iron doors that blocked the pit from above. After they had closed the opening from below with another lid, they came down. The heavy iron door in the first room was closed from the inside. After all entrances had been secured and checked once again, the blocked drain pipe and water flow were reopened. Now we could clearly hear the waste water flowing above us, and we knew we could not get out for many hours. We were buried beneath the sewers as if in a mass grave.

The noise died away. No one spoke.

A member of the committee said, "Please don't move about the malina; talk as little as possible, and avoid any exertion, for each activity uses additional oxygen. The air shaft was planned for fewer people; therefore, we must do everything possible to conserve oxygen."

The people were sensible and obeyed. Mothers gathered their children on the beds, and everyone sat down. My mother, Julek, Dolka, and I sat on our bed. Each of us thought our own thoughts. I looked about me.

Against the walls, on the long side of the hall, stood two rows of beds. Just across from us I saw the Feintuch family:

three brothers, with their wives and children. They were a nice family of large, quiet, pleasant people, totaling about twenty persons. Beyond them sat the "Małpes," a large family with three brothers and many sisters, all of them married with many children. They looked somewhat odd; their nickname fit them. They were very small and stocky, with strong hands and faces that reminded me of monkeys, but maybe that was only because of their nickname. The brothers had married equally small wives; even the sisters' husbands were small, although strongly built. Their many children were nice and jolly. They sat on their beds and played with all kinds of things they had been allowed to bring. I envied them and would have loved to play with them. Dolka took no notice of me and I felt all alone, but it was forbidden to speak or to climb down off the bed. So I just sat there and looked about me.

Next to us was another family. You could see from the men that they all belonged to the same family; they all looked alike. They weren't especially tall, but they were fat, and their wives and and sisters were fat—round, with round faces and round heads. I asked Julek about them. He said, "Those are the 'Kejkelech' chimney sweeps." That meant the "Balls." It was also one of the nicknames customary with chimney sweeps. The "Kejkelechs" had small children and two younger unmarried sisters. The mothers were playing with the children, telling them stories in quiet voices and nursing the babies.

In the corner across from us sat a young married couple with a fussing, newborn baby. Maybe he was ill. His mother was nursing him, but he kept crying until he fell asleep.

The hours passed; I didn't know if it was day or night. The two lightbulbs shed a dusky light. My mother suggested that Dolka and I try to sleep. I fell asleep.

Suddenly I was wakened by noise. Through the air shaft came the sounds of shouting and scattered gunshots from the outside. People pushed together toward the opening, but they were soon asked to go back to their places, because they were impeding the flow of air, and others would have trouble getting enough air.

Even after this short time a few people were suffering shortness of breath. The ventilation was so poor that some among us who were susceptible began struggling for breath. It was terrible to see them whistling as they sucked in the air; their faces became red, and they were slowly seized by panic. The doctor immediately gave them shots and pills; they quieted down and fell asleep.

Individual attacks could be alleviated, but the overall lack of oxygen remained a problem. In the meantime the shouts outside had faded. After it had been quiet for a while, it was decided to send one of the "Małpes" up the chimney, to find out what was going on. For a chimney sweep nothing is easier than climbing a chimney, but it was dangerous for him to look out. If he were to be seen from an upper window, we would be lost. A suspenseful silence settled over the malina. The man disappeared up the chimney, and scarcely any air reached us. Our nerves were stretched to the breaking point.

I huddled in my blanket and waited without speaking, like the others. But I was now getting very little air, and was afraid I would suffocate. Someone took me into the first room. When the "Małpa" came back from the lookout, he told us terrible things. Most of the inhabitants of the houses had apparently been taken away, and there were many corpses lying in the courtyard. It was quiet outside, but the "action" had probably not ended. In the distance he had heard screams, dogs barking, and many gunshots.

A decision was made to remain in the malina for a while longer. Those responsible began to distribute zwieback, margarine, sugar cubes, and water. Dolka and I ate in silence, but Julek, my mother, and most of the adults didn't touch the food. Fear was constricting their throats. Worry woke in their hearts for those who had remained in the ghetto above. Each of us had someone outside.

My mother didn't feel well. She was breathing with difficulty, and it turned out that she suffered from claustrophobia. She had never before been afraid of closed rooms, but now, walled up with one hundred eighty people in a narrow space, with no possibility of getting out, she suffered greatly. We were all concerned for her. The doctor took her into the first room, where there were fewer people and it was cooler. Perhaps there was also more air in there. I looked at my mother and I grew fearful. Her eyes were wide open; she was terrified, and appeared about to lose self-control. She took sedatives; despite them, she could keep from screaming only with difficulty. Her hands shook, and she broke into a cold sweat. Finally, the doctor gave her sleeping pills. She was put on the bed and fell asleep immediately.

After a long time noise and voices were again audible through the chimney. The Jewish police came into the courtyard and called, in Yiddish: "Come out to the trucks." This was targeted at those in hiding. The policemen were intentionally making a lot of noise to discourage those who had succeeded in hiding in closets and behind walls, so they would be frightened into coming out and joining their families. Finally they announced over loudspeakers that the Germans were threatening to blow up the houses suspected of harboring hideaways.

The noise outside had faded. But despair and fearful agitation prevailed in the malina. The children were feeling bored; some of them began to cry, and the crying was infectious. One after another began howling, and the adults were afraid the crying might be heard and betray us.

Suddenly the lights went out. The electricity had been cut off from the outside, in order to flush out people in hiding. We had an oil lamp and candles, but we couldn't light them because of the lack of oxygen. From time to time flashlights were turned on, but only as an emergency measure, and only for a short time.

We sat in complete darkness and held our breath. And then the entire malina began to tremble. The echo of a detonation reached us; we felt the earth shake and the change in air pressure. The explosion was like monstrous, ear-shattering thunder, followed by dreadful noise, like a never-ending landslide. We sat, bent over and petrified with fear. Everyone was horror-struck. It was evident that houses had been blown up, but we didn't know where. We had the feeling the building over our heads had been wrecked. Panic broke out; people ran back and forth in the dark. They demanded that those in charge open the malina immediately, to let them out. It would be better to die outside in the open air than to suffocate inside. They were calmed only with difficulty, but we knew it was impossible for us to get out immediately. Before the hole could be opened, the pump would have to be used for at least eight hours.

We heard screams from outside, and this noise gave us hope. The building had certainly not been wrecked, and our air shaft was still open. The committee pleaded with people to calm down. They adjourned to meet in the front room. The danger was clearly great; if the Germans had really learned there was a malina under the house, then sooner or later they would blow it up. We were afraid of being buried alive beneath the rubble.

But people can get used to anything. Most of the people calmed down, went back to their places, and waited for the committee to reach a decision. I lay down on our bed in the dark and immediately fell asleep.

When I awoke, it was quiet in the malina; only a baby was crying loudly. The light was back on, and those in charge were pleading with the parents to quiet the baby.

The mother rocked the young one back and forth and tried to nurse him, but he kept crying.

Suddenly voices could be heard outside. This time, there was no question: They were the voices of Germans. The people in the malina were afraid the howling of the infant would be heard outside, draw the attention of the Germans, and betray the malina.

We heard motorcycles, cries, and gunshots; below, with us, the child cried and screamed. People were demanding it be kept quiet. The father took his son, wrapped him up in a blanket, and covered him with a pillow to muffle his crying. Gradually, the child grew quiet.

We tried to follow what was going on outside. Then we heard a warning in German. Early next morning they would blow up the house. After that we heard a few more salvos of machine-gun fire and screaming, along with the sounds of cars starting up and driving away. Finally, it became still.

We were stunned with dismay. The committee went back to the front room for a further meeting.

Suddenly someone gave out a horrible shriek.

It was the mother of the baby. She was crying and screaming, tearing out her hair, and beating on her head with her fists. Tears streaming over his face, her husband was trying to calm her. A few people went to the couple's bed and picked up the baby, dead.

In trying to quiet the child and muffle his loud crying, the desperate father had suffocated his son with the pillow he had placed over his head. Everyone was rigid with horror. No one had wished this; no one had reckoned on such a thing happening. The thought was sad: that it might have cost the life of a child to save all our lives.

The small body lay in our midst in the stifling room. Hysteria began spreading, and then it was decided that we should leave the malina that night. The "Małpa" climbed back up. It took a long time until he returned. He gave us the news that he had been outside, and had looked down from the roofs. In his estimation, the Germans had left the ghetto, and the "action" was over for the time being.

Outside it was already growing dark. If they started to pump out the pipe sewage immediately, we would be able to leave the malina in small groups by daybreak.

When the exit hole was once again open, eight hours later, a terrible stench forced its way into the rooms, but with it came oxygen, so we could breathe easier.

The first to climb out were the men who would help the others climb out. This time a ladder was set up, for we had enough time to climb up slowly and quietly. The first out were the wretched mother of the baby, and the father, who carried his dead child in his arms. Following them were the weak and sick. Everyone else followed after them.

I was among the first, too, because my mother could hardly stand owing to the lack of air and the sleeping pills she had taken for the last two days. She was pale and weak.

Only when we got outside did we learn we had stayed in the malina a total of three days and four nights.

The ghetto lay there as if extinct; no person could be seen. Quickly and silently, we ran along under cover of the walls until we had reached our house. The doors were open, and the apartment was abandoned. We went from room to room in hopes of meeting someone, but no one was there.

We sat down on the beds and looked around us. The apartment had been left suddenly and in haste; everything was in its place; only the doors were open. In the first room the beds were unmade and breakfast dishes stood on the table. The bread was dry. Evidently our neighbors had had to leave their apartment immediately following breakfast, two or three days before.

The second room, ours, looked as we had left it: set to rights, and with the beds made. My school things lay on the table, where I had set them down after doing my homework. We had gone away in the evening, as darkness fell. I had not known that I wouldn't be going to school the next day because we would be in hiding.

I entered the third room, the last, for the first time. It was infinitesimally tiny. Here Rabbi Levin had lived with his family. Two beds, a narrow sofa, and a rickety clothes closet stood against the walls. A small window looked out on the courtyard; a second window, with a view of the street, had been walled up with bricks. From this window one could actually have seen out of the ghetto. It had been obstructed in order to deny us even a look at the "other side." Until then I had not known that our house was so near to the border of the ghetto, the border of freedom. The room, whose door had always been closed because of the rabbi's sick wife, smelled strikingly of people, medicine, and mildew. I knew the smell; I had noted it every time the door opened and the rabbi came out to fetch water from the kitchen, or to empty the chamber pot. Now the room was empty. Rabbi Levin, whom we had so treasured, was no longer there. When we had left the house to go to the malina, he had despaired and lost hope. My heart had told me that we would not see him again when we returned.

When Mother had collected herself, we washed up and changed our clothes. Then Mother wanted to go to Grandfather's house and look for her family. It was still dangerous to be out on the streets, because we didn't know if the "action" had truly ended, but Mother was impatient. Julek wouldn't allow her to go by herself; he wanted to escort her. But what would happen to me and Dolka, left all alone in an empty apartment in an abandoned house? After some give and take it was decided we would all go together.

My mother went out first. I followed her; Dolka came third; and Julek at the end. Grandfather's house was quite near, but the way seemed very long to me now. Again and again my mother stopped and took cover in the shadows of a door or an archway. Ducking from place to place, we advanced slowly. We skirted Rudnicka Street, the main street of the ghetto. In it was not only the Jewish Council, but also the headquarters of the Jewish police, directly across from the house in which my grandfather was living.

We climbed up the steps. It was alarmingly quiet. The big apartment, with all its rooms, usually filled with so many people, stood empty. Mother was so alarmed, she could hardly stay on her feet. She leaned on Julek and, abandoning all caution, called, "Papa, Papa!"

To our surprise the door of a closet in the corridor opened, and Grandfather crept out—small, weak, and very old. Never before had I seen him so small and so pitiful. His whole body shook; he couldn't say a word. With a trembling hand, he stroked my head. Tears ran down his face. Mother sat him down and brought him water, which he drank in one gulp. He didn't know where the remaining family members were. When the soldiers had begun to burst into the apartment, the inhabitants had fled in all directions. Left on his own, he had hidden in the closet. He was so weak and exhausted, we couldn't leave him there alone. So we stayed with him in the empty apartment.

After a while Lea returned; with her came Lena. They had fled through the attic into a neighboring house. There they had found a hiding place in a closed-up attic with friends of Lea's. They had heard and seen everything that had happened in the courtyard and in the house. They were horrified by the massacre the Germans had carried out in some of the apartments and in the courtyard of the neighboring building.

That evening Wolodja, Chassia, and Fejgele came back, too. They had succeeded in fleeing the ghetto through a hole in the wall, and in reaching the house at Number 1,

Zamkova Street, where they had previously lived. Unnoticed, they had crept into their former storage room in the basement.

For four long days the three of them sat, closed up in the small storage room. While they had had the advantage of not seeing or hearing what was happening in the ghetto, the fear of being discovered, and the cold and hunger, had been difficult to endure.

Two more days passed before we got news from Puszkarnia. Jechiel, Julia, and Jochele had reached the farm and remained there. They asked us to send them clothes, valuables, and money, so that they could pay the farmers who had taken them in. They also informed us they were going to stay there, and would not be returning to the ghetto.

That was the last news we got from them.

80

THE LIQUIDATION OF THE
VILNIUS GHETTO

IN JUNE 1943 a new name began to inspire fear among us: Kittel, a German officer and the head of the Secret Police for Jewish Affairs in Vilnius.

Kittel was a good-looking young man in his twenties. He was always elegantly dressed, and presented an extremely cultivated appearance. It was said he was an actor and musician, loved music, and played saxophone on the Vilnius radio. But behind his cultivated exterior lurked an especially subtle monster.

Kittel often came into the ghetto. He visited the workplaces, walked the streets, and entered the courtyards. When he met someone at work, he would praise him and offer him a cigarette. If the worker took the cigarette, Kittel would offer him a light.* If the man accepted the offer, Kittel pulled out his pistol and gave him "a light": He shot him.

Many stories of his terrible whims circulated about the ghetto. He had made his reputation by liquidating ghettos. They said he had already been responsible for the closing of many ghettos in the area, as well as for the horrible liquidation of the ghetto in Riga, the capital city of Latvia. Everyone in the ghetto was terribly afraid of this inhuman creature. Since Kittel often stopped by the courtyard of the

---

* Translator's note: In German, one asks for "fire" when one needs a light. Kittel was engaging in a gruesome and brutal joke by "firing" at a worker who needed a light.

Jewish Council, my mother wouldn't let me go walking there with my girlfriends anymore. With a heavy heart, I had to abandon my meetings with Judith Kugel.

A theater had been established in the ghetto, and my mother took me to each new production. Most of them were evenings of songs. The song texts were written by ghetto poets, and their themes reflected current events. Very soon I knew these songs by heart and sang them at home.

The "actions" took place more and more frequently. Anyone who hadn't yet found a hiding place, or who wanted to go to the partisans, was now using his last opportunity to flee. One ghetto gate after another was being closed.

The work crews—the "units"—were made collectively accountable for one another. If it was discovered that any members of a squad were missing (because they had succeeded in fleeing from the ghetto to the forests), the foremen of the unit involved, as well as their families, would be executed in Ponary.

Julek had to hide and—with some other men—once again climbed down into the malina for a time. Conflicts erupted between the ghetto police and the underground movements. The leader of the resistance, Jizchak Wittenberg, was caught and arrested, but shortly freed by his friends. The differences of opinion grew sharper between the Jewish Council, under the leadership of Gens, and the followers of the resistance movement, which my cousin Lea had joined. Kittel ordered the arrest of Wittenberg, but the underground fighters refused to give him up.

Fear ruled the ghetto and our nerves were stretched to the breaking point. The Germans issued an ultimatum: It was either Wittenberg or the whole ghetto. But even after Jizchak Wittenberg had surrendered to the Jewish Council and been turned over to the Germans, things didn't calm down. The ghetto seethed. The members of the underground movement left the ghetto in secret. All workers who labored outside were dismissed; all communication with the outside world was halted. The ghetto was completely cut off and was waiting for what would happen next.

We learned that Gens would have to hand over five thousand Jews this time. The terrible cruelty of this "action," conducted only by the Jewish police, appalled the inhabitants of the ghetto. Policemen forced their way into many apartments and dragged children and women out. We were lucky they bypassed our apartment. After this "action" everyone seemed crippled, and held their breath.

On September 14, 1943, a rumor spread that Gens had been arrested and taken away by Kittel himself. From some Poles, who had been pressed into service as cleaners for the Gestapo, we learned he had been shot on the very same day. It was now clear to all that there was no way to save oneself in the ghetto. The stress reached its peak. I, too, was conscious of this, and listened to all these stories at home. Again and again Julek and my mother discussed what they could do, but they found no way out.

We waited. Then the deportations began. Jews were ordered to leave their houses and gather for "resettlement in work camps in Estonia." Julek and my mother didn't believe this "resettlement." A few people had recently managed to return from Ponary, and Julek and my mother now knew for sure that the people who were taken from the ghetto were being led to their annihilation. They decided, as they had before, not to leave the apartment.

With Lena's consent, my mother brought Lea to live with us, for there was good reason to fear that the members of the resistance movement would be the first to be arrested and transported by the Jewish police. We hoped, moreover—thanks to Julek's connections—to save ourselves from being transported, and would pass Lea off as the third daughter of our family.

So began the "liquidation" of the Vilnius ghetto—its annihilation.

We passed the last night in the ghetto, the night of September 23–24, sitting on the marble steps of Number 6, Rudnicka Street, the house where the Jewish Council was situated.

In the entranceway, the passage to the first inner courtyard, there were two wide double doors, one on the left side and one on the right side. Earlier, before the war, these had been the main entrances of the erstwhile Yiddish Secondary School. The wide marble steps were decorated with all manner of statues and stone ornaments. On the steps of the right entrance my mother, Julek, Dolka, Lea, and I found a corner where we could sit down.

On the broad steps were ranged the last Jews of the ghetto: the "lucky ones"; the "privileged ones"; and the last ones to come out of their hiding places.

All who were here knew for certain they had no other choice, and had to give themselves up to the German bloodhounds. The time for flight had passed. My mother had refused to go back down to the malina, and then it was too late. Everyone who sat here had given up hiding; had had to leave their homes; and had already parted from their relatives. And so we sat, crowded close to one another, we "privileged ones" of the ghetto—the families of members of the Jewish Council and the Jewish police, the families of those who belonged to favored professions, or the foremen of work units; and the families whose hiding places had stayed undetected up until now.

Now we had all given up. We understood there was no more possibility of escape. We sat there and waited for the unknown. We sat on blankets or on coats and leaned our backs on the bundles and sacks of the few belongings we could carry. Only the essentials; what was necessary and indispensable.

Some time before, my mother had stitched a big canvas bag for each of us, with our names written on them for identification. The bags could handily be opened from the top. They had shoulder straps so we could carry them more easily on our backs. For one thing, this allowed us to move about better in the midst of a crowd; for another, it left our hands free to carry other baggage. With her free hand, my mother held on tightly to mine and made sure I didn't get lost in the crowd.

Not one of us slept that night. We sat there and looked about us and held hands. My mother stroked Julek's hand. Julek was very pale; a strange calm emanated from him. Even though we were still together, we felt we were taking leave of one another.

Each of us was lost in his own feelings and thoughts. There was a great crush of people, and no one dared leave for a second, for fear his place would be gone when he returned. Everyone waited tensely for new instructions. Some resigned themselves despairingly to their fate; others hoped for the mercy of heaven, and prayed quietly. Still others berated themselves for staying put instead of fleeing, to join the partisans and fight. And everyone was afraid. It was a creeping fear that froze the blood in the veins.

The staircase was only dimly lit; the long, narrow shadows looked ghostly and frightened me. Outside, it was pitch black. Silence reigned, but sometimes the cries of SS men could be heard as they discovered people and brought them here.

By dawn we were already so numb and in so much despair that we had hardly any interest in what was going on about us. We received the order to stand up and ready ourselves for departure; nothing else registered. We had resigned ourselves to our fate, and hoped only to remain together.

We were arrayed in rows of three and left the ghetto; it remained behind, empty. But soon the rows dissolved and we marched, in large and small groups, through Vilnius.

The streets lay there as if dead, as if the city were empty of people. Only a slight movement here and there could be seen, behind the window curtains of the houses we passed. We were surrounded by SS men with their dogs. The SS men bellowed and struck out with their clubs at anyone who happened to wander nearby.

We turned to the right, through Subocz; we went by the house in which Maisiei and my aunt Lena had lived. Full of sorrow and longing, Lea looked at her house. We marched on, along the street that led out of the city in the direction of Rossa.

The big Christian cemetery was in Rossa. To the left of the cemetery wall gate there was a fenced-in square, where the heroes of the nation were buried. Among them was the mother of Marshall Pilsudski. The heart of the great Polish leader also rested in her grave, as he had wished. He had loved Vilnius, his hometown, and the epitaph read: "Here lies a mother, with the heart of her son."

Near the cemetery the first selection took place. We were separated. The women, the children, and the old men went on to the cemetery; the young, healthy men were herded into the courtyard of a nearby house.

At the last moment, before he was separated from us, I saw Julek take a small package from his pocket and give it to my mother. She didn't want to take it, but Julek said to her, "Raja, take it; you'll need it. There are three of you and I'll be all right." Those were the last words we heard from him. We saw that this was good-bye. Four of us were left: my mother; the two girls, Dolka and Lea; and me, the child. We were pushed onward and taken to the cemetery.

The cemetery stretched out over a pretty hill; the graves were scattered over it. Between the graves wandered paths. There were trees and ornamental plants. The cemetery was surrounded by a thick, high wall. All the Jews of the ghetto had been assembled here. Some people had already been there three days, even old people and children. It was the last days of September, and the nights were cold. The ground was damp, and white with frost in the mornings. We got there on the third day of the ghetto's liquidation. When we came through the door, women were standing there searching the rows for relatives and acquaintances. Tired and depressed, our packs on our backs, we went with eyes cast down. We went along a winding path among the graves, looking for an empty place by a gravestone. While we were still occupied in taking off our packs and sitting down, we suddenly heard someone call, "Raja! Raja!" It was Lena's voice.

My mother ran in the direction of the call and saw Grandfather sitting behind a gravestone, his back against a rock. Next to him sat Chassia, with Fejgele in her arms. With outstretched arms, Lena ran to us and hugged Lea, her daughter. Crying, they kissed each other. Despite the sad occasion, they were happy to be together again. Wolodja and the other men had been separated from them two days before. The four of them had remained here, hungry and thirsty. Fejgele looked fearfully at me. The eyes in her small face looked especially big and black. She was sick. She must have caught cold in the nighttime chill and constant drizzle. Now she was burning with fever. Chassia was trying to comfort her. The little girl was thirsty; she begged for something to drink. But we had no water; we gave her rainwater from our hands. Grandfather sat there, gloomy and silent; he didn't react at all to his surroundings, and appeared to be barely aware of us.

So passed the hours. Our joy at meeting had faded, and my mother told them everything we had had to endure before we got there.

Lena was completely defeated. In the two days since we had seen her, the weak woman had grown old; it hurt her daughter Lea to see her that way. Over and over she said she should never have gone with us; she should have stayed with her mother. It was what her father had begged her to do before he was taken away. Now she was feeling guilty, as if she had betrayed the memory of her father in not fulfilling his wishes. She resolved never again to leave her mother alone.

Night fell, and we were out in the open, in the cold. Leaning on the gravestones, we sat on the cold ground and once again passed a long, sleepless night.

In the gray light of morning, a commotion was heard. Trucks with dozens of armed soldiers halted in front of the cemetery. First in German, then in Polish and Yiddish, a voice over a loudspeaker informed us that we should prepare to break camp and get into line beside the gate. Slowly, very slowly, people got up; one person after another; one group after another. Because there were thousands of people here, it was clear there was no reason to hurry. It would take us a long time to get into line; we had been sitting far away from the gate. From that direction came a racket: crying; blows; screams of pain; and the baying of dogs.

Lea started in that direction, to see what was going on, but she hadn't gone far when we heard loud cries coming down from the wall: "Jews, go to the right side, go to the right!"

Three young people, two boys and a girl, had climbed up on the wall and were running along it calling their warning down to the people in the cemetery below: "Go to the right!"

Shots were fired, but the three ran on to warn the people. Finally they were hit, but their cries could still be heard, until—one after another—they fell off the wall and were silent.

Those three young people, now dead, had told us important news, but the full meaning of it wasn't yet clear to us. We only understood that we must go to the right, at all costs.

We climbed up the hill in the direction of the gate; our packs were on our backs. Grandfather, Chassia with Fejgele in her arms, Lea with Lena, Dolka, and at the end of the group my mother, holding me by the hand.

It was laborious to make our way up the slippery paths among the graves; our feet often sank into the soft earth. A great mass of people was crushed tightly together in front of the gate. People screamed and shoved each other aside. The whole area in front of the gate was littered with all sorts of bundles; we had to climb over whole mountains of packs and baggage in order to move forward. Here and there old people lay among the bundles. They had fallen down and nobody was helping them. Soldiers with bayonets and rifles ran back and forth, shouting and hitting at people: sometimes with bayonets, sometimes with rifle butts.

The crowd pushing forward lost its bearings. Some were shoving forward to the gate, others pushing back toward the graves. My mother called loudly that we should stay together as tightly as possible. But we were soon separated. Grandfather stumbled and fell down; Lena helped him up and pushed him onward. Everyone's efforts to reach the gate went on; the nearer we got to the exit, the fiercer the struggle became. No one thought of others; everyone pushed and was pushed, with inhuman strength—the strength of those who want to survive.

Here mankind discarded civilization as if it were an article of clothing and left behind every decent feeling: love; loyalty; simply everything. Here it stood naked, and exhibited its wretched soul. Here, faced with the realm of death, all the baseness and cruelty of mankind was on display.

After an endless effort during which we fell down and stood back up countless times, we succeeded in pushing our way up to the cordon of soldiers. Here we paused for a mo-

89

ment; then we were shoved toward the left—toward the women over fifty, toward the old and weak, toward the children under fifteen years old. It became clear to my mother that you had to be young and strong to make it to the right. This was what the young people had meant; the young people who had warned us and who had died on the wall for us. They had shouted, "Jews, go to the right." They meant: On the right side is life. My mother stood still, collected herself, and wouldn't let herself be shoved farther to the left. She grabbed Dolka by the hand and with all her might shoved her toward the chain of soldiers. When the soldiers saw the teenage girl alone, they let her through. Dolka disappeared—to the right side.

The first task had been accomplished, and my mother was newly encouraged. She refused to go to the left but stood stockstill. She looked for Lea, and immediately grabbed her by the hand. But Lea resisted with all her strength, screaming, "No, this time, I won't forsake my mother." She followed Grandfather and her mother toward the left.

The faces of Chassia and Fejgele, of Grandfather, Lena, and Lea, disappeared in the crowd. We two stayed back, my mother and I, in the middle of the mass of shoving people. I fell down and couldn't get up because of the heavy pack on my back. My mother hauled me up, loosened the shoulder straps of the pack, and let it slip to the ground. She grabbed me tightly by the hand and pulled me back, through the cemetery gate and in among the graves.

It was difficult to prevail against the people streaming out; it took a long time, but at last we were back inside the cemetery. We caught our breaths behind an old gravestone. My mother considered what she could do. She weighed trying once more to conquer the wall of soldiers in front of the gate; the soldiers who separated right from left, life from death.

It was now all too clear to us that only teenage girls and strong women capable of work were being allowed to go to the right; old men, children, and older women were sent to the left. And that way probably led to Ponary, and to death.

After we had rested a bit, my mother pulled out of her pocket the little package that Julek had given her shortly before the separation. She opened it. It contained pieces of jewelry. She had another package like this one. On the day in the ghetto when the possessions of Jews had been seized, we had been ordered to turn over all our remaining valuables to the ghetto authorities. Grandfather had taken some watches and some gold to the Jewish Council, but my mother and Julek had kept their valuables. Now she took out the pieces of jewelry and gold coins and placed them in the pocket of her coat. We stood up. My mother was still wearing her pack on her back, and her hand was clutching mine in a grip of iron.

With a supreme effort we succeeded in conquering the forty or fifty meters (roughly 130 to 165 feet) that separated us from the gate. The soldiers were standing almost in the gateway itself; the selection to the right side began there. With me in front of her, my mother tried to shove through the soldiers in that direction, but one of them gave me a heavy kick and I fell to the ground. When my mother bent down to haul me back up, another soldier began to beat her with his rifle butt. In the tumult swirling about us, I managed to get up and slip back into the cemetery between people's legs. The pushing, the noise, and my fear were dreadful; now I had lost my mother, too. I began to scream and cry, but nobody noticed me.

It seemed to me an eternity had passed before I felt my mother's strong hand tugging me farther into the cemetery. She had immediately detected me among the many people and bundles, but it had taken some time for her to reach me. Those few minutes of being alone had stirred such a fear of death in me that I could do nothing but scream and cry.

We found a quiet place behind a gravestone. My mother dried my tears, calmed me, and ordered me to stand back up. We had to try once more to get past the soldiers. Her voice had changed; it was hard and cold, and it frightened me. I didn't want to go but was terrified of remaining alone. So when she stood up and pulled on my hand, I rushed and ran after her so as not to lose her.

We advanced only with difficulty. Among the bundles on the ground lay small children and infants who had been left behind, or who had been lost by their mothers. They cried and screamed bitterly. We ran on; sometimes we stepped on children and infants. They lay underfoot, and it was hard to distinguish between a bundle of clothes and a bundle with a baby inside it. Suddenly I noticed a baby directly in front of my feet. I stood still. I was unable to go on and step on the head of the child. My mother quickly hauled me up and over the baby, but I couldn't push from my mind the look on the face of the baby lying under my feet.

It was growing ever more difficult to get near the chain of soldiers. Many women were pushing at the gate; they wanted to break through the cordon and go to the right. Suddenly a bayonet hit me. I screamed with pain, and a warm liquid ran down my arm. I didn't stop to see what it was; I was trying to avoid the next blow. My mother gazed about her and saw the soldier who had done it. He was already beginning to raise his arm again. She turned to him very quietly and said, in Russian, "Drive us to the right, in the direction of the soldiers. For every blow toward the right, you will get a present." She pulled a diamond ring from her pocket and held it out to him. The soldier, a Ukrainian, understood the score at once, and agreed. Now it was easier for us to move forward.

The soldier shoved us to the right with his rifle butt; the others, to the left with his bayonet. For each nudge that advanced us, my mother gave him a piece of jewelry—sometimes a ring, sometimes an earring. He exerted himself and began to strike out forcefully. We quickly advanced in the desired direction; during the whole time my mother held my hand as tightly as a vise.

Beneath the blows, we reached the line of the German soldiers in front of the gate, but they wouldn't let us through and pushed us once again toward the left. My mother concluded we wouldn't make it that way. Three times now we had fought; we had stepped on others, and been hurt and stepped on, ourselves. And we hadn't succeeded in breaking through to the right. My mother felt her strength fading. She would have to come up with a new ruse, and quickly; time was pressing. The quota for those who would be designated as workers appeared to be filling up; fewer people than before were being allowed through to the right, to life.

We moved away from the din and pushed ourselves back into a corner, flush with the gate. All this time my mother never let out of sight "her" soldier, the one who had bullied us toward the right. He too was paying attention to my mother; he knew there were still more treasures concealed in her coat pocket.

This time my mother didn't allow herself even the smallest rest. It was almost twelve noon; soon the soldiers would take a break or be relieved by others.

We stood behind a tree. My mother took the pack from her back, opened it, and shook out its contents. Our clothes and last remaining possessions now lay on a grave near the tree. My mother held up the empty pack and ordered me to get into it. I didn't understand what she was planning, but there was no time to ask questions; I obeyed. She immediately pulled up the pack about me and closed it over my head. I bent down and squatted in the pack; I could feel her put on the shoulder straps. Then she lifted me high onto her back.

Once again my mother pushed back into the fight.

I felt the shoving of the crowd; sometimes I got hit by a blow from a rifle butt. It was dark and stifling in the pack, and my head whirled. Sometimes my mother fell down, and I felt the weight of her body on me. But she always got back up, and a heavy blow on my back drove her a few steps further. It was a hard fight, inhuman and hopeless; a desperate struggle that lasted about a half hour.

All of a sudden I felt ground beneath my feet, and could stand in a crouch. I heard my mother ask the surrounding women to push in closer to her, to shield her from the eyes of the SS officers. Then she opened the pack. We were standing outside the cemetery, in the middle of a group of young women, on the right side of the gate. Near Pilsudski's gravestone: a brave-hearted mother and her daughter.

We had won the fight for our lives. We were on the right side. The rumor of the girl in the backpack spread like fire among the women; many came to see me. Dolka came, too, and hugged and kissed me. There were a few friends of my mother's among the women on the right side, as well as her cousins Dora and Genia.

We were loaded onto trucks covered with green tarpaulins. We sat tightly packed into them, one next to another; one on top of another. On either side of the tailgate there were two long benches. Armed soldiers sat on them. They would guard us during the drive in order to prevent anyone from jumping down and fleeing.

We drove through Vilnius for the last time. We didn't see the streets through which we drove.

Then we reached the train station. There, on a side track, some distance from the station buildings, a freight train with several cars was waiting. Next to the track, along the whole length of the train, our escort stood—soldiers armed to the teeth. The soldiers fell on us with cries. A hail of blows broke over our heads, to make us submissive and stun us. But it wasn't necessary; we were broken and compliant. We hadn't yet forgotten the selection: the crying of those left behind; the children thrown down in front of our feet.

We knew that we would now climb aboard a train and be taken to a destination from which there would be no return. We were loaded into the cars, accompanied by shouts of "Hurry up, hurry up!" Once we were inside—about eighty people per car, squeezed together like sardines in a can—the heavy doors were closed and bolted from the outside. It was impossible to open them from the inside.

It was dark in the car. Only a little light came in through a small, grated hatch high above. A few women pushed their way to this opening and tried to look outside. My mother, Dolka, and I found ourselves in the middle of the car. We leaned on each other. The floor was cold, and we had no blankets. Other than Dolka's pack nothing remained to us. Now I really needed the winter coat that my mother had made me put on.

Whenever it had been dangerous, and we had had to move from one place to another, we had put on extra clothes; when we undressed, we shed one layer after the other, like onion skins. This made it possible for us to take extra clothes along without having to carry a bundle. I hated it, but now the extra clothing was all we had.

In the dark car, we pulled off the second set of clothing, as well as the second sets of underwear and stockings; we hoped that from time to time we could wash and change clothes, so as to keep a "tolerable" appearance. My mother's biggest worry was that we make a good, healthy, and "worthwhile" impression. She maintained this was the only way to survive, and had therefore done everything so that we would appear "presentable," at least on the outside. I was dressed well, and wore the best clothes that we had: a pretty green coat with a fur collar; comfortable, warm boots; and blouses and sweaters of good quality. This was reassuring to my mother; winter was already near.

Suddenly the cars started to move; we were off. It was night, and we were on our way to an unknown place, an unknown destination.

In the middle of the night the train slowed down and almost stopped, although it kept rolling. A few women pushed up to the little grated window. They looked out and announced, "Ponary."

A whisper went from mouth to mouth. Everyone knew this place—the place of death. It grew quiet; we held our breaths and trembled. Had we fought for this? Is this where our lives would end? Was this our destination—the end?

Some women became hysterical, and began to cry and scream. But the other women, whose nerves were stretched to the snapping point, couldn't endure the crying and screaming; they ended it with a few slaps. It grew still once again, and the wheels of the train kept rolling. Slowly, it's true, but they were rolling. The rolling lasted several minutes, then the train got underway. We breathed easier. We were going on. What had happened? Had all that been an additional torment, an additional cruelty and degradation? Were they trying to break us? No mind could grasp it; no human heart could believe it.

Underway, the train stopped several times. We didn't know why, and each time it stopped, we thought we had arrived. A few women immediately pushed their way to the hatch to try to find out where we were, but each time, the train began to move on after a short while.

Night became day. We were shut in, and there we lay, tightly crammed together without food and without anything to drink. In a corner of the car, we had found a cask in which we could relieve ourselves when we had to. But most of the time we just lay there; we slept or cried and thought of those who had stayed behind.

Memories were awakening in us. Most of the women were young—very young, at that—and had left their parents and their whole families behind. Now they felt their aloneness, and they were quietly crying and lamenting. It was even worse for the young mothers who had abandoned their children, and were now crying bitterly. They had lost their heads in a moment of danger, but now they were in great pain. They wouldn't let themselves be consoled; there were no words to comfort them.

I lay in my mother's arms. I hurt all over from the blows I had received during our attempts to win through to the right side. The bayonet cut on my arm hurt especially. My mother comforted me and talked quietly with me. I asked her how those mothers could have thrown away their infants, there on the heaps of bundles. My mother tried to explain it to me. She said, "Susinka, they are young; it is important they survive. Together with their children, they had no chance to save themselves. The war will pass; the horror will end; and these girls and young women will have new children. It will be good; they will be free and happy. And never forget, you cannot judge them. No one may condemn them who hasn't been in their situation."

There in that car, on a journey into the unknown, I learned that people in extreme situations can behave completely differently from the way they usually do. No one can know how he would himself behave. Many who give the impression of being strong might allow themselves to become discouraged, and weak ones might become heroes.

Where Genia and Dora sat, in another corner of the car, there was a stir. During the whole trip some women had been trying to pry a plank up from the floor. Now they had succeeded in taking out two narrow boards; an opening to the outside lay before them.

They began discussing who was ready to flee through the opening. Most of the women were afraid; others feared being punished because of any who fled. They wanted to hold back those who were willing to flee. After long deliberation it was decided that all who wished to could jump. If their escape succeeded, the Germans would learn nothing of it, since we had not yet been counted and entered on lists. If the escape failed, they would imperil only themselves. Five courageous young women decided to jump; Dora was among them. "Good-bye," she said in Russian; she squeezed herself through the opening, and disappeared.

The train went on. We heard some gunshots and didn't know if the women had succeeded in escaping. The wheels rolled on.

Another day passed, and still the train went on. It stopped in the night a few times. At one of the stops, the door, which had been fastened from the outside, was suddenly ripped open. Two men sprang up into the car and immediately stretched themselves flat on the floor among us. It was quiet for a moment; then one of them struck a match, as if he wished to light a cigarette; the other asked, in Russian, "Do you have matches?"

The women didn't understand; the two *had* matches. But I was an inquisitive child who had always listened attentively, and I understood the question. I nudged my mother. She held her hand over my mouth and said, "Be quiet and lie down." The men lay there silently for several minutes. Then they asked again if we had matches, and when they got no response, they tried to persuade us. "Are you certain that you have no matches?"

The fearful women said nothing. The men quietly climbed out of the car and closed the door from outside.

The train started up again.

I remembered hearing, at home in Vilnius, that the partisans' correct password this year was "Do you have matches?" Those in the know had to respond, "Yes, we have matches."

I asked my mother why she hadn't answered the men with the correct password, and she answered that it had been dangerous. Furthermore, the partisans would not be interested in us, and especially not in me.

The trip into the unknown went on.

We later learned that, at the time of the ghetto's liquidation, about ten thousand Jews had been living there. The young men were sent to Estonia, to work camps. Among them were Julek and Wolodja. We women—about seventeen hundred of us—were taken to Kaiserwald, near Riga, Latvia. All the others—the sick, the women, the children, and the old people—were sent to Majdanek, to immediate extermination. Among them were:

Grandfather Schmarjahu Indurski;
Chassia and Fejgele Indurski;
Lea and Lena Nowogródzki;
Grandmother Weksler, Ljuba, Elke, and little Hella;
Schejndl and Sarale Weksler;
my mother's old aunt, and her grandchildren Lonja and Natasha.

All were members of my close family.

After a few days in Kaiserwald, I wrote the following poem:

I walk along my streets,
all's still and mute around,
they seem so foreign to me,
fearful, I gaze about.
Where now are all my friends?

Where have they gone away?
Why did they rob me of them?
It fills me with dismay.
I walk, and still, my heart cries,
although I have no tears;
through my whole life there will be
no joy, but only fear;
throughout my life, no luck
will ever come again.
I want to weave my freedom,
and spin away my pain.
I never will forget
the minute of despair,
even though I should be peaceful,
and goodness be my share,
the dreadful scene will stand
before my inner eye.

And then my heart, in weeping,
will break into loud cries.
And when I would expel
the scene with horror filled,
it comes right back to me,
more awful, and more wild.
It returns and comes back to me
in more dreadful mold.
And when it has gone by,
it still does not grow old.
It still is so near to me,
it makes my heart to bleed,
so without joy or courage,
I look on all I see.
Just hate and disillusion
have brought me to this plight:
for me, there's no more sunshine;
for me, there's only night.

KAISERWALD

TOWARD MORNING we arrived at the camp.

The cars were opened noisily. We could hear dogs barking, and loud cries of "Out, out!"

After three days and nights in the train it was hard for us to stretch our limbs; they had turned to stone. But the soldiers drove us on with blows and cries that rang in our ears like the barking of the dogs. While the first people were jumping down from the cars, soldiers climbed in and began to hit and shove us. I was thrown from the car and fell on the wet earth. I got up only with difficulty, dizzy, and with my legs hurting.

We breathed the fresh air deeply. The stench in the car had been terrible. We were in a thick forest. None of us knew where we were, but somehow we had a good feeling; we soon believed we had left the worst behind us.

The whistle of the locomotive sounded; the wheels turned, and the train left the forest. My mother clutched my hand. It hurt and I tried to pull it away from hers. Dolka walked behind us, sad and distressed.

The women carried the personal belongings that still remained to them. We had nothing anymore; my mother held on to me. Only I remained to her.

We were warm; the many pieces of clothing we wore weighed heavily on us. My green winter coat with the fur collar was appropriate neither for the mild weather nor for the surroundings. But my mother wouldn't let me take it off.

We were lined up in rows of five and marched along the

railway tracks. A large, nicely decorated iron gate appeared before us. Behind it stood several charming white houses with flowerbeds. Orderly white-graveled paths wound among them. Two mastiffs lay beside one path. We went in past the well-kept houses, and then through another gate. Here the scene changed. Behind this gate were a couple of large gray houses and a big, empty, gray-paved square with a column in the middle of it. In front of our rows of women, SS officers were standing and scrutinizing those who went by. Our unit was stopped and one of the officers called, "Sisters?"

Uneasiness grew among us as the two sisters who were standing in the first row of five were separated and sent to two different halls.

My mother let go of me and sent Dolka into the row behind us. We went on. Suddenly the officer pointed at us and bellowed, "Mother and daughter?"

I heard my mother answer, loudly and decisively, "No."

We were given instructions to leave our things on a heap in front of the entrance of one of the buildings and go inside.

The building, a blockhouse, was very large and empty. In the right corner there were thin straw mattresses heaped one on top of another. Two women SS overseers roamed about the blockhouse, shouting. They wore uniforms and black, shiny boots. In their right hands they carried whips, with which they struck out at everyone who came within their reach. When no one was nearby, they snapped them against their boots. Here they were known as "blitz maidens."*

My mother took a thin, dirty straw sack and ordered Dolka and me to do the same. She tried to find a place

---

* Blitz maiden: In the jargon of National Socialism, female SS supervisors were officially called "Female Intelligence Assistants." Girls over seventeen were exhorted to join up voluntarily ("German girl, the SS force is calling you!") in order to free up men for battle. Prisoners in the camps called the female supervisors "blitz maidens," perhaps because of the lightning-shaped insignias on their uniforms.

among the other mattresses on the floor, but there was little room remaining. The mattresses lay the length of the block-house, so that five long, side-by-side rows were created, with no passage between the rows. My mother and I lay in the middle of the third row and Dolka in front of us, in the fourth.

There were more women penned up in the blockhouse than there were mattresses; many more women than the blockhouse could actually accommodate. We had to crowd together and lie back to back. We pulled off our coats and jackets and laid them under our mattresses, together with our shoes. Outside, behind the blockhouse, there were wa-ter faucets and the latrine, which was actually just a ditch. A few women went to the latrine; since nothing bad happened to them there, other women went out, too, to wash and re-lieve themselves. My mother whispered to me that we would wait a bit. She asked Dolka for her soap and towel, for we had neither; when it got a bit darker, we also went behind the blockhouse. It was nice outside after the heat and stench in the blockhouse. My mother led me to a dark corner, so that no one would see me, and undressed me. My body was black and blue from the blows, and I also had some open wounds on my arms and legs. I hurt all over. Slowly and carefully she cleaned my bruises; then she washed herself. She had wounds on her back and shoulders, too, and I tried to clean them carefully.

I had a lot of difficulty with the fact that there were no separate toilets. It was hard for me to relieve myself in front of others, even when I had to go really badly. My mother stood in front of me and tried to shield me, but I could barely urinate. When we got back into the blockhouse, it was already completely dark. We stepped over sleeping women, trying to be careful, but it was difficult to find places to step among those lying down. Finally, after much fumbling in the dark, we found our mattresses. But the space had become smaller in the meantime. In the terrible crowding, the women next to us had commandeered almost our entire space. My mother lay down in the narrow crevice that remained; she pulled me over her and then wedged me down until a narrow space between her and her neighbor had been created. I fell asleep.

Shouting, commands, and the barking of dogs tore me cruelly from sleep. I didn't understand what was happening, where we were, or what I should do. Before I managed to get up from the mattress, I was knocked down by the women about me who were trying to stand up and run to the end of the blockhouse.

Everything was happening lightning fast. SS men had entered. They were beating us awake with their rubber truncheons and herding us to the end of the blockhouse, where a barrier had been erected by putting up a cable. We stood there, as tightly packed together as we could be; but the SS people kept pushing and shoving. Women larger than I were standing, or—to be more accurate—leaning on each other, back to back. But I, who was smaller, saw nothing. Bodies reared above me; I got no air. I had no room; even the space above me was occupied by the arms and shoulders of those standing. I let my arms sink, folded them against my body, and made myself as thin as possible. Then I tried crouching down to withdraw from the tightness and pressure and immediately felt a strong hand with long fingers and pointed fingernails dig into my hand.

It hurt badly. I wanted to scream. Perhaps I did scream, but my screams were swallowed up by the bodies about me and the general hubbub. My hand was forcefully pulled upward; I had to stand on tiptoe and stretch as far as possible and even further than that. I raised my head and looked into my mother's eyes. Her brown eyes, that could smile so gently, were serious and commanding. I understood. I must stay standing and be tall—as tall as everyone else!

Hours went by. It was hot; it stank. We were sweating

and thirsty, but still we stood, packed tightly together, a tangle of bodies. Over and over, people stepped on my feet, elbows hit my head, and I was struck by shoulders. But I remained standing. It wasn't really standing, actually, because I was squeezed up among those around me; I couldn't have bent over even if I had wanted to. And still we were pushed up even tighter against the wall.

The women were called out for registration, one after another. We—that is, my mother, Dolka, and I—were standing in the middle of the breathing mass, and it took a very long time until it was our turn to step to the desk where registration was taking place. We went together. First, my mother gave her particulars; then it was my turn.

Name: Susie Weksler

Born: in Paris

Date of birth: 19 . . .

"1926," said my mother quickly.

So I had suddenly become seventeen; six years older.

I didn't yet understand why, but a look from my mother made me keep silent. Then it was Dolka's turn. She gave her particulars, and we were allowed to go back to our mattresses. We had gotten numbers 5082, 5083, and 5084.

I went back to my mattress. Suddenly I noticed that my boots had disappeared. My mother ordered me to keep still; the Germans were still in the blockhouse. When the Germans left, she would begin to look for my boots.

I was terribly scared. I had no other shoes; I was barefoot and it was cold outside, and the courtyard was strewn with sharp gravel. More than anything else, though, I feared my mother's temper. Only when she had composed herself, with an admonishing look, did I feel somewhat safer.

My shoes were nowhere to be found; I had to go barefoot across the courtyard to get the thin soup we were given for breakfast. My mother was crying.

Miraculously, after eating, she found a pair of beat-up

shoes someone had thrown into the corner. I tried them on. They were too small for me; besides that, they had high heels. I had never before worn high heels; I found walking in them tough, but I had no choice.

Sitting and lying on the floor, we waited.

The Germans, the officers, and the blitz maidens went to the blockhouse next door, after our blockhouse had been registered.

The large blockhouses in this section of the camp were used for the intake and registration of arriving transports. The women from our transport had been divided up among three blockhouses. The whole area was known as "quarantine." Anyone here didn't work, and got only one ration of food per day.

It was quiet in the blockhouse now, and in the ensuing pause, we looked about us. My mother noticed acquaintances, her cousin Genia among them. She came over to us and sat down beside us on the mattresses, and began to tell us her story in a quiet voice. She, her mother, Dora, Lonja, and Natasha had all been taken to Rossa on the first day of the ghetto's liquidation. They had been at the cemetery for three days together, and Dora had cried the whole time. My mother was surprised that Lonja was at Rossa; half a year earlier he had been living with a Polish woman outside the ghetto. But Genia told us that Dora hadn't been able to stand the separation from her son. The last time she went to see the boy, the Polish woman hadn't allowed her to see him, for fear the boy would blabber and endanger her.

Dora reproached herself for having given her son to a stranger. One week before the liquidation of the ghetto, she left it secretly, met with some Polish acquaintances, and told them the whole story. They advised her to leave the boy with the Polish family until everything had quieted down. They even went so far as to promise her to fetch him from the woman if it became necessary. But Dora didn't listen to them.

With the help of a Jewish policeman from the ghetto, Dora forced her way into the apartment of the alarmed Polish woman. She grabbed her son and took him with her back to the ghetto. Shortly afterward the liquidation began. At the selection in front of the cemetery, Lonja, together with his grandmother and cousin Natasha, had gone "to the left." "That's why Dora jumped from the train," said Genia. "She was certain that, if she succeeded in escaping, she'd also find a way of saving her son." Genia wept quietly. Now she was alone, and frightened for Dora. My mother comforted her, and Dolka invited her onto her mattress, so she could stay with us.

Night fell, and we were hungry and exhausted. Suddenly a woman came up to us. She knew my mother from Vilnius. Hesitantly, and obviously fearful, she asked her, "Are you the former proprietress of the Bon Ton?"

"Yes."

"We found something, and the women said it belonged to you."

"Me? What? I don't believe I've lost anything."

"Psst . . . Here, in this small packet."

From under her blouse the woman pulled out a small gray sack that was bound with string. She opened it and showed it to my mother. It contained pieces of jewelry. I glanced at the glittering contents and thought I recognized Julek's ring. But my mother turned her back to me and wouldn't let me see the things. She was probably afraid of being betrayed; at any rate, she said, quietly, "No, that doesn't belong to me. I already turned my valuables over to the Germans."

I looked about me and saw many faces turned to us. I didn't understand. My mother pushed me onto the mattress. I leaned back and wanted to ask something, but she only said, "Quiet, now, go to sleep."

Again, I didn't understand. I wasn't sure whether the

things belonged to my mother or not. If yes, why had she lied? No one had spoken with me at all since we had left the ghetto. My mother only gave me orders, and the other women were occupied with their own concerns.

In the course of the evening I saw that there were a few more children in the blockhouse. Two were about as old as I; one was even younger. I also saw some older girls. But we stayed close to our mothers the whole day, and didn't dare approach each other, or even look at each other.

It hadn't yet gotten late when I heard crying in the darkness of the blockhouse.

"What's going on?"

"Be quiet; those are the poor mothers," said my mother. She, too, was crying quietly. Not far away from us I saw three sisters from the "Kejkelech" family. The eyes of the older sister were very red, and the other two sisters were caring for her. I then remembered that one of them had had small children; children with whom she had played in the malina, in the ghetto. I immediately understood. The poor woman had left her children on the left side.

During the night I was awakened a few times by loud crying. I heard shouts in German, and twice I also heard gunshots. But my mother had obviously covered me so well that I didn't take in everything that was going on. I fell asleep again.

It seemed to me that I had hardly slept, when we were awakened. It wasn't yet light outside; it was probably four in the morning. We were chased out into the courtyard.

"Roll call."

Hurry up. Hurry up. In the dark—always five women side by side—we had to line up in long rows. Straight rows. Adjustments to the left or right. Stand at attention and don't move. I was tired; besides that, I wasn't used to standing in place, motionless. My mother pleaded with me, commanded me to stand still, or I would get a blow on the head from one of the women SS overseers.

We were counted: once; twice. Again the rows were straightened up. The blitz maidens reported to the officer on duty. They conversed among themselves.

A fine rain fell. We stood there. The ground became wet; it began to turn into cold mud. And still we stood there. The blitz maidens were dressed well; they wore black raincoats and boots. But we had barely had time to get dressed; now we stood there in the rain, wet and shivering from the cold.

When it got light, our food was brought into the court-yard. We were very hungry. During the whole train trip, four days long, we had received not a morsel, and yesterday evening's soup had really been more cloudy water than soup.

A big kettle containing a white, sticky, sweetish mush was set up in front of the blockhouse. From now on this thin stuff would be our breakfast, for as long as we were in the camp. We stood in line; each of us got a gray tin plate onto which a small portion of the disgusting stuff had been slopped with a ladle.

Naturally blessed with a good appetite, and now starving, I began to eat at once; but Dolka refused to touch the stuff. My mother ordered her to eat it, but without success. She stubbornly refused, and it came to a fight, as it so often did. Dolka maintained that since she was almost nineteen, she was grown up enough to know what was good or bad for her. With her father now not here, she was no longer going to take orders from her stepmother.

Relations between my mother and Dolka had been very tense the whole time. Dolka resented my mother for letting her go alone to the right side and retreating with me, the previous week. In her eyes, my mother had left her in the lurch. She was feeling very abandoned there, without her beloved father and among all these women and girls, none of whom she knew.

My mother was in despair. What was she supposed to do? When all was said and done, she had a moral obligation to look after her stepdaughter; but how would that be possible? And then there was me, constantly crying in the past few days. My mother finally blew up at me and told me to shut up already, howling over any little thing.

We ate outside, in the rain, and even then we weren't allowed back into the blockhouse. We were given an order to turn over all our watches and valuables. Two women in striped clothes that reminded me of pajamas went from woman to woman, carrying a basket. They were accompanied by threatening-looking blitz maidens. The women had to put their watches and wedding rings into the basket. Not much was collected; most valuables had already been surrendered in the ghetto. My mother took off her watch, but I knew she still had some things hidden.

Next to come was bathing and disinfection, which was called "delousing." Only then would the women be taken to the main camp or the workplaces farther off.

Again we were lined up in rows, three women across this time, and we went to be disinfected. I distinctly felt the nervousness and fear about me, but I didn't know why.

We went through the gates and came to the cared-for part of the camp with its flowers and fountains. Then we took a turn to the left, until we came to an inner courtyard. There we had to stop and wait. After a time additional groups of women from other blockhouses in the transit camp arrived, but we weren't allowed to approach them. I saw several women crying. I recognized two of them; they were the sisters who had been separated. When the courtyard was full, the roll call began.

Again we stood in rows of five, an unending number of

rows the width of the courtyard. German officers and guards roamed among us, counting us again and again, straightening the rows, and making jokes with each other. They even went away for a while and came back again, and we had to stand still.

Standing so long was very difficult for most of the women. After a while the first ones began swaying. Some fell to the ground. Immediately, blitz maidens were upon them with their whips; they hit or kicked a swaying woman, until she stood upright again, or fell entirely to the ground.

This second roll call of the day lasted five hours. In the future I would stand outdoors many, many times: in the heat and in the cold; in snow and rain; by day and by night; and I never understood what all the standing was good for other than to satisfy the sadistic inclinations of the camp supervisors. The blitz maidens were the worst; they would administer a beating at the slightest provocation.

Now things were moving a bit. Slowly, slowly, in groups of fifty women, we were taken to the washrooms. Everyone was afraid; only I didn't know yet what was coming or what could happen.

My mother was especially tense; she looked about her on all sides. I felt she was looking for any way to prevent my having to go into the washroom, and I understood her anxiety. Only healthy, strong young women were brought to this camp, and I was a child, which would be readily apparent in the washroom. Amid the frightened crowd of women, and constantly concealed behind my mother's back, no one had noticed that I was a child up until now. But what would she do with me in the washroom, a place where everyone undressed and was exposed to the gaze of the blitz maidens? Then it became clear that the women who entered the washroom were not returning to the same courtyard. We had no choice, then; we had to go in. My mother spoke with several women she knew from home and asked for their help. And those women who, a short time before, had survived the liquidation of the ghetto, the cemetery in Rossa, the terrible selection; those lonely women who had only just lost their own children, promised to help my mother. They had no definite plan, but I felt, all of a sudden, that there were other women besides my mother who were caring for me and protecting me.

With a group of women, we entered the first room, gave our names in turn, and received a tin badge with a number on it. This badge hung on a string that we had to fasten around our necks. Each of us then received a clothes hanger.

We had to go to benches that stood against the walls. When ordered, we began undressing and neatly hanging up our clothes and underwear. We had to hang the clothes hangers on wall pegs. We could take only our shoes with us. Then a door opened, and two German officers appeared, with billy clubs in their hands. They yelled, "Get out! Get out!" and pushed the women on so that they had to pass by them. My mother said, "Stand up straight, head high; you've got to look big!"

The whole group tried to form a tangle in order to quickly move on together, without drawing the attention of the SS people standing there.

It worked! Together we went by them, and they didn't notice me. My mother pulled me closer to her and kept a lookout.

We went through a long corridor and into another room. Men in camp clothes stood there; prisoners who were called "convicts."* I thought I heard them called "striped ones" and imagined they had that name because of their

---

* Translator's note: A play on words in German. "Sträflinge" (convicts) sounds similar to "Streiflinge" (striped ones).

striped clothes. In front of each of them there stood a stool. The blitz maidens yelled at us to sit down on the stools. We did so, holding our shoes in our hands. Before we understood what was happening, the men began to cut off our hair with clippers. Terror. Silence. Nobody said a word. The men worked as if they were ashamed to be dressed among the naked women: they, the convicts, shaving the heads of women, new convicts; cutting off their tresses, their hairdos, their ornament, their glory. Not infrequently, a shaver slipped and wounded a scalp. The prisoners were trying to hide their shame.

One after another we went into the next room. There, naked and shorn, we had to wait until the whole group had gathered and was ready to shower. Next to the door, we put down our shoes and huddled together, not only because there was little space in the room, but even more out of despair. Each woman was seeking comfort in the proximity of her sister, and from a feeling of shared fate. I couldn't see myself, but the shaved heads of the women around me terrified me. At first I couldn't recognize anyone. I was alone; I couldn't even recognize my mother. Scared, I began to run among the women. A woman took my hand, but it took a while before I recognized her as my mother. She was silent. She said not a word, and her wide, gaping eyes had a look I had not seen in them up until now. By the force with which she held my hand, I sensed that she was trying to overcome panic; that she was once more trying to marshal her remaining forces and stay strong.

I didn't recognize Dolka at all. My stepsister wasn't pretty. We all knew it, even Dolka herself. She was large and clumsy, with big hands and feet. She had a healthy, full-figured body, although she wasn't fat. Her face was plain, too, although her features were straight and normal. Dolka had a hard mouth, heavy, plump cheeks and a straight nose. Her nose was too long in relation to her mouth, which was accentuated by a jutting jaw. Her eyes were brown and not large, and set somewhat apart. They emphasized her extremely high forehead. Dolka was always sad; even when she smiled, sadness was in her face. I never heard her laugh aloud or sing. Her only beauty was her hair: black, heavy, and lustrous. Dolka was always trying out new hairdos and changing her appearance.

Now I couldn't recognize her at all at first. Her head looked even longer. Her skull arched up high and looked like a big egg. Her appearance repelled me. Dolka seemed to know how curious her skull looked; she withdrew into herself. She was ashamed, and was afraid of looking at anyone. After a time I pulled myself together and went to her and hugged her. Dolka took me in her arms and laid her curious head on mine.

In some way I loved Dolka, although our relationship had always been superficial and she had never played with me or looked after me when my mother was out. But we had slept together on a single bunk, and sometimes at night I would hug her and snuggle close. Although I was the smaller one, I pitied her because her mother was so far away and because she had never gotten to know her. I also understood that she was disadvantaged in comparison to me. Because she was the elder, she was always having to give in to me.

We went into the next room. At the entrance, each of us received a piece of soap. On the ceiling of the room were many showerheads. The floor was made of gray stone or something that looked like stone. It was very slick and wet. The first women to enter the shower room lost their footing and fell down. We went carefully, but despite that, my mother slipped. A few women helped her stand up and my mother was frightened, which wasn't at all like her. Then we stood under the showers and waited. Suddenly ice-cold jets of water came spurting out. The women shrieked, and tried to move out of the way. My mother commanded me to wash myself, despite the cold water.

"Soap yourself; soap yourself well," she hissed between her teeth.

Suddenly the water became warm; then a boiling-hot stream came down on us. The women crowded against the walls; some got burned nonetheless. The water temperature fluctuated again, and after a while it became comfortably warm, so that we could wash ourselves. All at once I saw my mother take something from her mouth and try to press it into her soap. She also pushed something into my hand, a ring, and ordered me to press it into my soap as I washed myself. Dolka got a ring, too. I succeeded in pressing the ring into the soap and in concealing the hole remaining with soft soap.

Just as suddenly as it began, the stream of waters stopped. Several women hadn't managed to rinse off the soap. Again we heard shouts: "Get out! Get out!"

Still wet, we went to the exit. There, a camp inmate gave each of us a dirty rag that was to serve as a towel. We dried ourselves off and went naked to a table standing in front of us. Behind it stood women in prison clothes. They each gave us a specific item of clothing: underpants, undershirt, dress, headscarf, and jacket.

The convicts were silent and sad, but they smiled at me. They tried to give me clothes that fit. They had immediately perceived that I was a child. In their eyes I noticed the same motherly look that had accompanied me since morning.

"Hurry up, hurry up!" shouted the blitz maidens; they helped us on with their whips.

Still wet and only half dressed, we stood in a back courtyard that was filling up. We were waiting for the next group coming from the shower room. In the meantime we looked about at each other.

In the last few hours we had changed a great deal. We

had no stockings, only our wet feet in our shoes. Our gray-blue striped clothes and jackets were either too big or too small for us, as if we were playing dress-up. Our heads were shaved slick and were wounded from being shaved. Everything seemed so odd to me that the impulse to laugh took hold of me. I could hardly recognize my mother, let alone her cousin or my stepsister, they were so changed. Even their facial expressions were no longer the same. I had the feeling of standing backstage at the theater, surrounded by alarming-looking, costumed actresses.

Some years back—I wasn't even six yet—when all was still right with the world in which we lived, I had gone with Michla, my governess, to the Yiddish theater. We sat in the front row and waited for the curtain to rise. The master of ceremonies came down in front and asked, "Children, is there anyone among you who can recite a poem by Kadje Molodowska?" She was an author who wrote in Yiddish for children.

I sprang up and shouted, "Me!"

Immediately hands reached out and lifted me up on the stage. The master of ceremonies asked which poem I wanted to recite, and I said, *"Di dame mit dem hintl."**

It was a long poem, but after a few seconds of panic and some stuttering, I set out and declaimed the whole poem. It was a great success. The children in the house applauded, and the master of ceremonies gave me a kiss. I was taken behind the curtain and the actors gathered about me. Then I got scared. The actors were made up, and their strange, painted faces and ragged costumes frightened me so much that I began to scream. I could scarcely be calmed down. I don't believe I even stayed to see the performance. I only remember my family used to say that for a long time, I would wake up screaming at night with bad dreams. Again

---

* *Di dame mit dem hintl* (Yiddish): "The lady with the doggy."

and again the terrible picture of those made-up faces rose before me. My mother consulted a doctor; only after I had been given medicine would I gradually calm down.

Now, as I considered the women about me, I remembered my earlier fright. But this time there were no costumed actors.

When the courtyard was full, we were arrayed in rows of three, counted, and then marched to the camp. This time we were led through a side gate, passing the transit camp on our left. Back there, in the blockhouses, were our last possessions; things we had brought with us from home. We went through another, heavily guarded gate and along a narrow lane between fencing and barbed wire. At the end of the lane we reached a small gate, in front of which stood a single guard post.

We entered a wide square, around which stood large blockhouses. The blockhouse entrances were on the narrow sides. In all there were five blockhouses. In the middle of the square was a special place for wooden food kettles. The whole area was secured with double strands of barbed wire and electric cables; guards stood on watchtowers at all four corners. On one side of the courtyard, the side bordering the woods, I saw narrow train tracks and the autumn forest. Opposite, there was a gate in the fence through which you went to get to two smaller barracks that served as an infirmary. Farther off could be seen another fenced-in courtyard with blockhouses about it; that was the men's camp.

We were divided into five groups and taken to the blockhouses assigned us. We—my mother, my stepsister, Genia, and my mother's friends—were in Blockhouse 2. There were already other women in the blockhouse. For the first time we heard the name of this place: Kaiserwald. Later we learned that only four hundred women from Vilnius had been taken to this camp. The other women from the transit camp were sent to workplaces outside the concentration camp. We never met most of them again; sisters who had been separated heard no more from each other.

Before the war Kaiserwald had been a holiday resort. Well-to-do families rented cottages and passed the warm-weather days here. There had been all kinds of colorful flowers here, wide lawns, rivers and beaches, and wonderful walking paths in the forests.

The forest was big, dense, and dark; a variegated forest, like all the forests of the east. Among the trees were layers of fallen leaves and pine needles. In autumn the forest was cold and damp, but in summer many red and black berries grew there, and—when it had rained—big, meaty mushrooms shot up from the ground.

In the middle of the resort stood a big, beautiful, comfortable hotel for guests who had come for only one or two weeks. It had a large, white-painted wooden porch; the guests sat on it in the afternoons, ordering drinks and all kinds of cakes and pastries. They listened to the orchestra or danced on the square in the evening. The rich people of Riga loved this beautiful, peaceful place, and many Jewish families had been regular visitors.

Now there was a camp for forced labor here, and SS Lieutenant-Colonel Sauer stood at its apex. The lawns had been paved and had become roll call grounds. Only the hotel had been preserved—a memory of earlier, nicer days; the command headquarters were in it. The pleasant atmosphere of earlier days had given way to a tense mood. Instead of the quiet chitchat of yesteryear, loud, coarse voices and bellowed orders were heard; instead of dance music, German marching songs. And the elegantly dressed public of former days now wore uniforms.

The new masters drank much wine and beer, and the smell of schnapps* hung in the air. Instead of the refined

---

* Translator's note: Schnapps is a type of distilled liquor similar to brandy.

and well-dressed women who had earlier stayed here, there were now quite different women running about: the blitz maidens. You only ever saw them in uniform. Their blouses were tight and accentuated their breasts; their knee-length skirts were tight, too. They wore ties and silk stockings, and black boots with high heels. The tailored jackets were tight and short and also emphasized their full breasts and their narrow waists. You could tell that most of them went in for gymnastics, riding, and sports, as was demanded of German women in those days. Their hair was cut short, and blond; their faces were pale, and even their eyes and noses looked as though they had been cut from the same pattern. Their gaze was arrogant and hard, with lips pressed together. The blitz maidens always carried whips in their gloved hands, like experienced riders. I began to think that some of them never walked on the floor. When they entered a block-house, they immediately sprang up onto the long table that stood between the double-decker wooden bunks. They shouted their commands and cracked their whips in all directions. When I stood on the floor, I was very afraid of them. But when I sat up above on my bunk, the whole act looked comical, and reminded me of a circus, with the SS woman as lion tamer.

As we were entering the blockhouse, a woman SS overseer sprang up on the long table and gave orders that four women were always to occupy each bed. Two rows of double-decker bunks stood against the long sides of the blockhouse—always two, side by side, with a small passage in between them. Therefore, on each level, eight women lay in two bunks beside each other. In each bunk there were two pillows and two blankets.

My mother, Dolka, Genia, and I climbed up onto an upper bunk. We were lucky; the bed stood beside the window. Each of us had the towel and soap we had received at the showers and nothing else.

The blitz maiden pointed out to us the blockhouse commando: Karola, a kapo* who had been arrested for prostitution and theft; she wore a black insignia on her prison clothing. From now on she would be in charge; everyone would have to report to her whatever occurred. She would also distribute the bread, the margarine, the jam, and the drink at supper. For each bunk supper would be four portions of army bread, perhaps two or three centimeters (about an inch) thick, on which had been slapped a bit of margarine and a dab of beet jam. Everybody also got a cup of lukewarm tea. The few knives allowed us were firmly attached to the middle of the table. My mother divided her bread ration into four very thin slices; she also cut my portion and smeared two of the slices with margarine and two with jam. She took one of her margarined slices, ate it slowly, and drank the tea with it. She gave me two slices of bread, one with margarine and one with jam. She ordered me to eat slowly, so that the food would last longer in my mouth and satisfy me longer. The remainder of the bread she hid under the pillows.

Genia was watching my mother. She smiled and—like my mother—divided her bread in two. She ate one portion; the other she stored. Only Dolka ate all her bread at once, and my mother didn't dare to give her advice. But before we went to sleep, she said, "Dolka, tomorrow you will be very hungry again."

We slept two on each end of the bunk, our feet by the heads of the other two. My head lay almost on my stepsister's feet. In the neighboring bed slept four acquaintances of my mother.

Rachel Krinski was a big, broad-shouldered woman with

---

* Kapos: Concentration-camp prisoners who supervised work crews of prisoners without working themselves. They were mostly professional criminals, often extremely brutal, and answerable only to the SS squad leader.

long, beautiful legs, a pale face, and a self-assured gaze. Rachel had left her only daughter, a three-year-old girl, in Vilnius with a childless Polish family. She yearned for the child, but consoled herself that the little one was in a safer place. She had no wish other than to survive this hell and to return to her daughter. Rachel, an educated woman, had worked at the J.W.I.* She spoke a good Yiddish and immediately became attached to me.

Marila Krinski, her sister-in-law, was a small, gentle woman who wouldn't let Rachel out of her sight. Her husband, Engineer Krinski, had always pampered his wife; without him, she was now lost. The couple had had no children, and she showed no understanding for a child like me who lay beside her.

Fienia Wolkowyski was a pretty, refined woman, very calm and patient. Her husband, a doctor, had been separated from her in Rossa; their only son, Alexander, was with him. Fienia didn't know where the two men had been sent, or if they were even still alive. She sighed and cried a great deal.

The fourth, Dascha, was the youngest of them. She had married shortly before the war, and while the Russians were in Vilnius, her husband had proposed she travel with him to Eretz Israel. Dascha's husband had succeeded in getting a certificate, an entry permit to Eretz Israel for himself and for his wife. But Dascha hadn't been ready to part from her parents in the middle of the war. Therefore, they had decided that he should go on ahead, and that she would follow him in a few months. But she got no opportunity to do so. When the Germans occupied Vilnius, Dascha and her parents were taken to the ghetto, where her father died a year later. Finally, Dascha had been separated from her mother in

---

* J.W.I.: The Yiddish Research Institute in Vilnius; center of scholarly research into the Yiddish language and literature. Today the J.W.I. goes by the name of YIVO Institute for Jewish Research, and is located in New York.

Rossa, and now she was here, in the concentration camp. She was very quiet and spoke little. Her mother tongue was Polish; she hardly understood Yiddish. She was a tall, beautiful woman, slender, with brown skin like velvet, very large, dark eyes, and a full red mouth. In the first days in the camp she was already trying to exchange her bread for cigarettes. She smoked a lot; it was more important to her than food. I wondered how she had joined up with the group of women next to us, but the three older women cared for her as though she were a younger sister.

This is how our new daily routine ran: Wake up at three-thirty A.M., while it was still dark outside. After personal business—standing in line for the faucets and the toilets, making beds, dressing—all women were standing on the roll call ground by five A.M. Roll call lasted varying amounts of time. The blockhouse kapos counted the women who stood outside in straight rows, checked the blockhouses, and counted the sick or the dead in each blockhouse. When the counts were tallied, the ceremony of reporting to the blitz maiden began.

Then the officer on duty arrived and received the report of the SS overseer. From here he then went on to the other camps: the general men's camp, the camp for criminals, the camp for Jewish men, the infirmary, and so on. If everything was correct, and he was in a good mood, he then gave us the order to stand at ease; but sometimes the roll call stretched out over many hours.

After the roll call we waited in a long line before the food kettles, which stood in the middle of the courtyard. One after another, we got a ladleful of yellowish mush on our tin plates. Since we had no spoons, we slurped the stuff from the plates. Afterward we returned to the blockhouse to clean the plates and put them on the table.

On the first day of our stay, we found on the table yellow Stars of David with a black "J" printed in the middle, along with white strips of cloth, blue crayons, and black ink. There were also needles and thread. The blockhouse kapo selected two of the new women to assist her. Since we spoke Yiddish, Polish, and Russian, and she was a German, she couldn't understand us. Her two helpers spoke a bit of German and served as her interpreters.

Each woman sewed a Star of David on a white strip of cloth. With the black ink, the two helpers wrote the woman's number on her strip. This badge was sewn on the front of the outer clothes, on the left side, at the level of the heart. I sat up on the bunk and observed the scene. My badge was sewn on by my mother.

At twelve noon the soup was dished out: a thin, gray cabbage water in which a few grains of barley floated. After that there was another roll call at which the women were assigned various jobs. My mother, Dolka, and I were assigned to working on the railroad tracks.

We left the camp on foot and marched perhaps twenty minutes to work. We had to carry heavy rails from one place to another. My mother took care that I was in the middle of the heavy iron rails, at a spot where the weight was less heavy. At five-thirty we went back to the camp, where there was once again a roll call. After that we got our bread ration at the entrance to the blockhouse. At seven the lights were turned out.

The days went on like that, and we accustomed ourselves to the new way of living. Hunger grew worse and food became our primary worry. The few children in camp stayed in the blockhouses. These were children of Jewish families from Hannover, who had come to the camp months before we had. But even in our transport a few mothers had succeeded in smuggling their daughters to the right. The girls didn't get up for roll call in the morning; they also didn't go to work. During the day they played behind the blockhouses and waited for their mothers to return. My mother granted my wish and let me stay in the blockhouse, too.

One evening a woman came over to us. Inge had already been in the camp for a long time. She came from Hannover. Her family had owned many stores there. A year ago she, both her daughters, and other German Jewish women had been taken to the ghetto in Riga. The women were divided up among the houses, and could hardly believe their eyes; the ghetto was empty. Shortly before they had arrived, the Jews had been taken from their houses and deported on trains. The "action" had taken place around midday, and the people had been taken from their dwellings as quickly as lightning, while they were eating lunch. The dishes and glasses still stood on the tables; even the freshly prepared meals.

The Jewish women from Hannover settled themselves into the Riga ghetto, but after a few months they were brought to the Kaiserwald concentration camp. Inge had come here with both her daughters: one my age, the other, somewhat older. In the first days of their stay in the camp, Inge and her older daughter had gone to work and had left the little one in the camp with the other children. But one day, when they returned, most of the girls were nowhere to be found. Inge's youngest daughter was among the missing. Inge was now warning my mother that she shouldn't leave me alone, but should take care that I was "useful." "Here only those who work have a right to live," she said. After that warning, my mother woke me up next morning and dressed me, and I went to work.

My sleep was troubled, and I was constantly tossing and turning. The bunk was narrow for four women, and I wasn't letting my neighbor sleep quietly. At night I kept trying to raise my arms and stretch my legs, and so I would bump into my sleeping neighbor. None of the women wanted to sleep next to me. My mother tried to have me lie on the edge of the bunk, but even that was no good; because of my restlessness, I fell out of bed from the upper tier, and woke up half the blockhouse.

I was getting hungrier day by day, but other than the rations we received, there was nothing to eat. And although my mother gave me a large portion of her ration, it wasn't enough for me.

My mother was getting thinner and thinner. The work on the rails was hard. The farther the rails were laid, the more distant we got from the camp; the march to work became longer and harder. Sometimes, when the guards weren't watching, the women hid me among the building materials and the iron sections so I could rest a little.

When I wasn't working, I crept into a corner and sang quietly to myself. The working women heard my quiet singing and got accustomed to hearing me. Sometimes, in the evening before lights-out, they asked me to sing. Then I softly sang songs in Yiddish. Some women joined in, and so I learned more songs, among them songs of the Vilnius ghetto. Our blockhouse kapo liked to hear us and allowed us to sing from time to time.

Every morning when my mother woke me up, I cried. I was naughty; I didn't want to get up; I didn't want to work. It was late autumn. We worked out in the open, in rain and wind. I froze and got wet, especially my feet in the ragged shoes, which were too small for me anyway. My feet were so cold that sometimes I could hardly feel them, but my mother ordered me to go to work with her, and she wouldn't reconsider.

One day we came back to camp especially tired. That day the guards had not allowed us even the shortest break. At noon we hadn't gone back to the blockhouse as we usually did, but had gotten our soup at the worksite. We had to carry the heavy track rails farther than usual to lay them on prepared ties for the men to secure with big hammers.

When we came back to the camp, it was almost dark already. This time we didn't go to the blockhouses and we didn't receive our bread ration. Instead we had to stop on the roll call ground. This was unusual, especially when it was so late. We were afraid.

When it had gotten completely dark and the searchlights had been turned on, the "at ease" order finally came, and we could go into our blockhouses. At the entrance each got her bread ration. It was actually somewhat larger than usual this day. We laughed and were glad. But suddenly we noticed something was missing, and then we knew what it was. A couple of the little girls were no longer there. The poor mothers began to cry and scream, but then the lights were turned out. "Quiet," someone shouted, and it was all over.

After the "action of the children" my mother was very tense. Each morning at roll call she kept her eyes peeled, looking for a way out.

In the blockhouse next to ours a mother was living with her two daughters: One was a year younger than I, the other older. Batja, the elder, was working with us on the rails. Her mother had been working in the camp up until now, in the group that helped to clean and maintain it.

Two days after the "action of the children" Batja's mother joined us to work outdoors. Batja and her mother were dismal and constantly crying. I asked Batja where her sister was, and she burst out crying. Her mother told us in a tear-choked voice:

"On the day of the 'action' all three of us stayed in camp. My heart told me something would happen, and I wanted us to stay together. I left my younger daughter in the blockhouse and ordered her to stay between the beds, so nobody could see her from outside in the courtyard. I was cleaning the latrines with Batja when the truck drove up to the roll call ground, and we heard the Germans shouting. I ran to the blockhouse to check that my daughter had hidden herself well under the bunks. Then I went back to work. The Germans entered the blockhouse; they had dogs with them, and the girl got scared and started to cry. The SS people found her immediately and took her to the truck, along with six other girls they had found. I ran out and fought with the soldiers, who were holding me back from climbing into the truck. My daughter was weeping, and she cried, 'Mama, Mama.' A blow from a billy club knocked me to the ground. At the same moment I heard my bigger daughter, Batja, weeping. She came running out of the blockhouse and helped me to stand up. Both my daughters were crying, 'Mama, Mama, don't leave me alone!' one on this side, the other on that. I had to choose.

"I was looking at my big daughter. She is just thirteen, and she was crying. I knew I had to look out for this daughter, so she could maybe stay alive. Moreover, I knew I could do nothing to help the little one; she had been condemned to die in a few hours. I chose my bigger daughter; perhaps I can help her to stay alive."

My mother was crying. And I—I didn't understand how this woman could have let her little daughter go alone. I grabbed my mother's hand and pressed myself close to her, but my mother whispered in my ear, "Go back to work, quickly."

Our camp was overcrowded. Blockhouses that had been built for two hundred women each now held about five hundred. Most went to work outside the camp, but some still remained back in the camp, and did some senseless tasks; they carried stones from one place to another, for instance, or cleaned up the leaves in the forest.

The days passed by and became shorter, and the nights became very cold. The blockhouses weren't yet heated; the iron stoves that stood at the blockhouse entrances weren't yet in use. We also had no wood. Mornings were especially cold; when we went out, the ground was still frozen with the night's frost.

One day many SS people we had never before seen suddenly showed up at the roll call ground. We stood rigidly in the cold, but we hardly felt it; it was clear that something was about to happen once again.

And indeed, after the exact count and the regulation report, the strange officers walked among the rows and selected women. Each woman pointed at had to step out of her row and join a group that stood to one side. A German approached the row in which I stood. My legs began to tremble and I was afraid I might fall. My mother was standing in the row in front of me. The German passed by me and pointed to Dolka. Dolka's face fell, but the blitz maiden immediately came and hit her with the whip and took her out of line. I held my breath. My gaze met Dolka's eyes and I could see the fear crying out from her. So Dolka was separated from us.

The Germans went by me and pointed to Genia. Genia didn't wait for the whip; she squeezed my hand lightly and went. Six hundred women were taken away on that day. They left the camp, collected in various groups. After the "action" was over, the kapos stepped out in front. Each was carrying in her hand a stick with a sign, on which was the name of a temporary work commando. We received the order to line up behind the respective kapos.

Helga was the daughter of Genoveva Maier, one of the Jewish women from Hannover. She came to me, took me by the hand, and led me to a group headed by her mother. She was carrying a sign that read "Anode Factory."

I was dazed; I didn't know what I should do. I looked at my mother. But her gaze was wandering about. Suddenly our gazes met, and I saw she had tears in her eyes. She nodded to me as a sign that I should go with Helga and Mrs. Maier.

The groups began to move; my mother stood motionless in her spot. We went through the gate. I turned about and looked at my mother; I didn't know what I should do. The group went on; I went with it.

We left the camp and immediately turned to the right, toward the transit camp. From there, we went along a lane between the two men's camps, to the rear exit of the camp. A little farther on, by the edge of the forest, there stood a building; about it lay piles of big batteries. This was my new workplace.

In the anode or battery factory, as it was also called, no batteries were manufactured, but exactly the opposite: They were taken apart. Only a single barracks was situated in the broad terrain between the camp and the forest. Beside it ran narrow train tracks. Whole trains—freight cars and flat cars—arrived along here, full of big, used batteries, the kind you use for automobiles. We offloaded them from the cars and laid them down by the tracks. After the sergeant in charge had checked the shipment and had earmarked the batteries slated for dismantlement, we heaped them up in various stacks. About thirty women were working here. We brought the batteries into the building. A group of women who sat at a table dismantled the batteries into single parts; there were usually six parts. At another table, women broke down those parts further, into their components.

Around five in the evening the women from the battery factory returned. Once again we walked between the two men's camps. Dozens of men stood watching us on both sides of the road, behind the barbed-wire fences.

The men on the right side wore various chevrons on their striped clothing. I saw black triangles: felons; lilac: clergy or sexual deviants; red: political prisoners. The triangles also displayed various letters: F meant Finnish; LT, Latvian; L, Lithuanian; N, Norwegian; R, Russian. Those without letters were Germans whose citizenship had been taken away. This was the international men's camp.

On the left side was the Jewish men's camp. The prisoners wore a yellow star with a J in the middle.

It turned out that a group of Jews from Germany was

here—from Hannover, Cologne, and Düsseldorf. Our forewoman, Mrs. Maier, had a husband and a son in the men's camp. They saw each other every day when the women went by their camp. The men called out something to us in German, but I didn't understand them.

I found my mother in the blockhouse. She lay on the bunk and stared at the ceiling. She was gloomy and worried about Dolka. I climbed up onto the bed. My mother looked at me and was startled. I was black from head to toe; my hands and my clothes were dirty; my face looked like a chimney sweep's. My mother pulled herself together and climbed down from the bed with me. Before I could eat, we were going to the washroom.

The blockhouse was long and narrow. A narrow corridor stretched past the entrance door. On its right side was a door to a room in which there were five or six toilets. These were toilet bowls with no seats; next to each bowl was a water bucket. The bowls stood opposite one another, and so we always had to do our business in the presence of other women sitting on the toilets opposite. Next to the door was a water faucet, from which you drew a bucket of water to flush the toilet. There was no paper.

Across from the toilets was the washroom. In the middle of the room was a water pipe with eight faucets, four on each side. The water ran into a trough that looked like a rain gutter laid on its side. There were wooden benches against the walls.

To get to the toilets, you had to pass the door of the blockhouse kapo. When we went by, we reported: Number So-and-So is going to the toilet, or Number So-and-So wants to wash herself. If you didn't speak up, the blockhouse kapo might come out and hit you with the whip, or report you to a blitz maiden. The punishments could turn out to be severe.

As we went by the door this time, my mother loudly

called out our numbers and where we were going. The door stood open. The blockhouse kapo looked out. She saw me, black as I was, and started to laugh loudly. She came out. We were scared, but she scrutinized us and laughed happily, asking what had happened to me. She gave us an extra piece of soap, for me to wash myself with.

All in all, Karola, our blockhouse kapo, had an agreeable temperament; she was cheerful and nice. She had taken on the job in order to improve her living conditions and to get additional food. She was no supporter of the Nazis, and her relationship with the prisoners was as good as was possible given the circumstances. But even she wasn't always friendly. In the presence of the blitz maidens she was angry; she shouted and was severe. But as soon as the Germans had left the blockhouse, she tried to help insofar as it was possible. She had a lover, a German prisoner arrested for murder; when the lights were out, he visited her in her room. He was a kapo in the men's camp, and had taken the job to improve his own living conditions. He behaved more humanely than the other blockhouse kapos, too.

Karola entered the washroom. I had undressed, and my mother was helping me to wash myself. She took care to shield my naked body from the eyes of the German. Only a small light was burning in a corner of the dim room, and Karola stood there.

Karola told my mother that the people who had been taken away in the past days had been taken to work at I.G. Farben.* She had heard it from her lover. My mother seemed to take a new lease on life. We finished washing in record time. We went back into the sleeping area and

---

* I.G. Farben: Former German chemical company, established by the merger of the BASF, Bayer, Hoechst, Agfa, and other companies in 1925. This company, like other industrial ventures, established branch factories near concentration camps, because the prisoners could be utilized as slave labor, with a small per capita fee paid to the government.

climbed up onto our bunk. My mother whispered to Marila and Rachel what she had learned from Karola, and the news spread like wildfire. The women were excited, and one pleaded, "Susie, sing us 'Vilnius.' " I began to sing quietly. The women listened; first they cried, then they quieted down.

My mother had changed greatly since the day Dolka had left us. She seemed very quiet and far away; she slept little and cried a lot. Because she had lost weight and become weak, she could no longer work outside at track building. When an officer showed up at the roll call ground one morning and called for workers for the clothing depot, she stepped forward. So a new period began for us.

My mother was working in the clothing depot. The officer in charge of the clothing depot was a tall young man with a narrow face and soft, wavy, dark hair. He wore an SS uniform, riding breeches, and black boots. My mother told me he knew much about art, and could immediately single out any valuable items from the things that were brought in. For that reason he had been transferred to the clothing depot. I didn't know his surname; among themselves, my mother and the other women called him only "Hans." He loved classical music; when he was present, soft music was always playing in the clothing depot. He was an educated man and behaved in a friendly manner to the women who worked for him. He seldom shouted, and had outbursts only when he was drunk.

He didn't like having to look at the prisoners' garb the women wore. Therefore, the women who worked for him changed and wore civilian clothes of their own choosing. They were allowed to select these clothes from among the things on hand. For this reason, the women working there also found it easy, from time to time, to smuggle out an additional piece of clothing under their prison garb. When they left the clothing depot to bring in or take out laundry during the day, they wore their prison uniform, with their number and the Star of David, over the other clothes.

Hans mostly took his meals in his office in the barracks. The leftovers—and sometimes they were not a little—he left on the table. He would call one of the women to come clear the table off. This woman could keep whatever was left of the food, and could also share some of it with the other women in the clothing depot. Therefore, my mother felt she could sacrifice her food ration in camp and leave me her bread and her soup. She also brought food with her into the camp, and I felt somewhat fuller at supper.

We were now in deepest north-European winter. It was icy cold and snowing. When we went to work or stood on the roll call ground, we were very cold. Our feet grew numb; our hands were red and swollen. We had no change of underwear, and so we washed our things every evening and laid them out to dry on the ends of the beds. In the morning, when we put them on, they were still damp and frozen stiff. When the cold was unendurable, the stove would sometimes be lit in the blockhouse, but we hadn't enough wood. What we had sufficed for an hour only, and that was too short a time to warm the poor wood barracks with its stone floors.

The women removed wooden planks from the bunks and burned them. But more than a few planks per bunk could not be taken out, or the mattresses would have inadequate support and would fall down. When the blitz maidens noticed that a mattress wasn't lying straight, they immediately checked the planks. If some were missing, then the women who lay on those bunks were hit and—as punishment—had to kneel on a stool on the roll call ground for a long time.

My mother secretly began to smuggle in various things from the storehouse, under her clothing. These were things that the inmates had brought with them when they had come to the camp. The chests and bundles left on the roll call ground of the transit camp were taken from there to the storehouse. Besides those things, articles from Jewish homes in Riga and its surroundings, and from the homes of people arrested for political offenses, were also delivered there.

When the storehouse became full, shipments were sent to the German Reich. From time to time packages of presents were sent to officers and important civilians. The officers at the camp also sent packages from the storehouse back home. Valuables were immediately forwarded to the Reichsbank.

My mother was dividing, sorting, and making an inventory of the things that came to the clothing depot. Sometimes she found foodstuffs like zwieback, sugar, and jams. She risked her life bringing these things to the camp and dividing them with her neighbors or giving them to others who had pressing need of them.

Sometimes she smuggled out a piece of clothing concealed on her body, and so gradually, the majority of the women in our blockhouse were able to exchange their underpants or stockings for better ones. Warm headscarves were also greatly desired. It was December, and very cold on our shaved heads. Most of the women who worked outside had colds. They suffered from ear infections and similar conditions. Besides that, all the women had wanted to hide their bald heads immediately after they were shaved. Some ripped up a shirt, a blouse, or simply a towel in order to cover their shaved heads. The Germans who were guarding us also suffered from the cold and found no fault with our new head coverings.

My mother also brought me a pair of shoes. It's true they were worn down and too big, but they had leather soles, and so my feet wouldn't get wet anymore when I walked through the snow.

One day my mother brought a bra, cotton, and even

some rouge. She was now waking me a half hour before reveille each day. I climbed down from the bed, went by Karola's door, loudly called out my number, and went to the toilet. It was the only time when I could be alone, and the only time I could relieve myself. In the presence of other women I was unable to. When I didn't succeed in emptying myself in the morning, I was unable to for the whole day. I then washed my face and hands and cleaned my teeth with my finger and some soap. My mother paid special attention to this; she firmly believed that cleanliness would protect me from illness. When I got back to the bunk, the women were still asleep, and my mother began her work. She dressed me in the cotton-stuffed bra. I was the only one in camp who possessed a bra, and yet I still had no breasts at all. Only after this was I permitted to dress, and my mother began to put me to rights. She smeared some rouge on my cheeks so that I would look healthy and strong; then she artfully bound a cloth about my head as if it were a turban. Over this turban was put another headscarf, which she tied like a grandmother's kerchief.

The cloths were gray, to avoid attracting attention, but the special way they were fastened made me look older and a few centimeters (an inch or two) taller.

When we went to roll call, I looked like the other women: thin, but as tall as they were. I had always been a big girl, but now my mother checked me each morning and wished that I could grow up faster. And—miracle of miracles—despite the tormenting hunger and the hard living conditions, the wish appeared to be working. I was getting taller every day.

My mother was dedicating all her thought and strength to "organizing" survival necessities—"organizing" is what theft from the Germans was called in the camp—and I felt neglected and somewhat alone.

After almost half the women in our blockhouse had

gradually been moved to a more distant work camp, bunks became available. Niussia, with her daughter Rafi, moved into the bed beneath ours. Niussia knew my mother from Vilnius. Her husband and his sister had been friends with my mother and her brother. I knew Niussia from the ghetto, too, because she, her sister-in-law, and her niece had lived there together with my best friend, Judith Kugel. In the overcrowded blockhouse I had not noticed Niussia until now. I had encountered almost no acquaintances, and Niussia was especially quiet.

She was a beautiful, energetic woman. I don't know how she had succeeded in escaping having her hair cut. But the fact was, I had seen her reddish-brown locks peeping out from under her head covering. She always bound her headscarf especially tight, so one couldn't see her hair. Only at night—or to be more exact, in the mornings, when I got up before everybody else—did I see her curls. Niussia was in her late twenties; she had remarkably narrow hips and, despite her gauntness, beautiful, full breasts. Her face was pale, but under the paleness one could still see a rosy gleam. Her skin was young, smooth, and soft as velvet, and appeared almost transparent. She had a straight, somewhat pointed nose, and a sensuous mouth with full, red lips. Her eyes were big and green, with long, dark lashes. And added to this was her hair. It was reddish-brown, and the heavy, shining curls fell luxuriantly onto her shoulders. Her walk was proud and beautiful, with her head held high.

Niussia stood out from the other women, something she wanted to avoid at all costs; to be conspicuous brought only troubles here. It was much better to disappear into the gray multitude. But Niussia had a further reason to be inconspicuous. Her daughter was seven, the only little girl left in the camp. I don't know how she had succeeded in bringing her daughter to the camp, but she was there—unregistered, without a number, and without having gone through disinfection. She didn't wear the camp uniforms, either, but her normal things from home, and she got no food rations.

Right from the beginning Niussia had worked in the clothing depot, for that occupation was easier, and she could find something to eat there for Rafi, her daughter. She was also the one who had advised my mother to volunteer for this work.

In the morning, when Niussia and my mother went to work, the little girl stayed under the bunk, even in bed sometimes, under many covers, so no one would see her. She wasn't allowed to leave her hiding place, not even to go to the bathroom. She had to lie there, still and quiet, until her mother came back.

Once or twice in the course of a day, the women in the storehouse came back to the camp: to fetch blankets to be disinfected in a rectangular wooden chest; to change mattresses; or to fill old mattresses with straw.

Each time Niussia came back to camp, she secretly entered the blockhouse to see how Rafi was doing. From the very first day she and my mother were working together, they became very friendly, and did almost everything together. They came to the camp carrying the heavy blankets to and from their disinfection. While they were doing so, they smuggled in whatever food and clothing they could as well as—most importantly, and most dangerously of all—medicines.

There were also doctors among the inmates. They had brought medical instruments and the most essential medicines with them in their bags. Sometimes the women also found painkillers and prescription medicines for diabetes and heart and asthma ailments in the bundles of clothes that came to the storehouse. They would then smuggle these medicines into the camp and hand them over to the barracks in which the Jewish sick were housed.

A few doctors who were also camp inmates worked in

this sick barracks. In the fall of 1943 Dr. Bolek Lóczak arrived. He was a doctor who had worked in the Polish underground and been arrested. We called him just Dr. Bolek. He was a young man, tall and good-looking. Before the war he had been known as a brilliant doctor. Now he was responsible for the sick barracks. It was no normal hospital. The sick—men and women from the camp—stayed there only a few days. If they weren't healthy again in two or three days, they were taken far away from the camp, and the rumor spread that they were killed in the forest. Dr. Bolek wanted to rescue as many ill people as possible, but to do so, he needed medicines, shots, bandages, and salves.

My mother, who had gotten very weak after the "action" in which Dolka was separated from us, had begun to vomit and to suffer from terrible stomach pains. One day, when she could no longer stand the pain, she turned up at the dispensary next to the sick barracks. It was her luck to be examined by Dr. Bolek. The doctor grasped that she was suffering emotionally under the separation from her stepdaughter. He understood that the sleeplessness, the vomiting, and the stomach pains came from the guilt my mother felt, although she was not to blame. Her feeling of responsibility for the girl who was gone (a responsibility that her beloved husband had transferred to her), and the feeling of having failed, gnawed at her.

Dr. Bolek was a wise man who wished to save people. He perceived that he couldn't help her, but he attempted to do so by means of psychology. He proposed a certainly dangerous but very responsible action to my mother. He convinced her to risk her life to try to smuggle as many medicines and medical instruments into the sick barracks as possible. And so my mother and Niussia began to bring the medicine they found in the storehouse into camp.

Each day, when I came from the battery factory tired and dirty, I got soap from my mother and sometimes clean clothes, too. After roll call I washed myself, came back clean to the blockhouse, and received my bread ration. I was now allowed to eat the whole ration in the evening.

In the morning, in addition to the sweet mush, my mother gave me a piece of bread from her own ration. At noon I got an additional bowl of soup from Karola or my mother. I wasn't so hungry anymore, but I was always ready to eat everything that I got my hands on. Now that I was fuller and drier and had clean and warmer clothing, I had the time and desire to look about me.

Winter was now at its height, and it got dark early. By four P.M. we were already returning from work. I was visiting Niussia's daughter when I made the astounding discovery that the "girl" was no girl, but a boy—Rafik—in girl's clothing.

A small, thin, pale seven-year-old, Rafik hadn't left the blockhouse since the day of his arrival more than three months ago. His reddish hair was short, and he was very pale. Rafik had become accustomed to staying still; he was always silent. Sometimes I thought he was mute. I spoke to him, telling him what was going on outside. I was trying to befriend him, but in vain. The boy was so terrified and withdrawn, he reacted to absolutely nothing.

Niussia liked to see us together, so I passed most of the time before lights-out in the lower bunk, with Rafik. My mother and Niussia sat up above and busied themselves with their own concerns—the smuggling of medicine and clothes, and how to obtain additional bread.

In the time I was together with Rafik, I began making poems again. At first it was only a few words for Rafik that rhymed or were funny, but over the course of time they grew into verses.

Rachel Krinski was the first to take notice. She proposed I say the poems over and over; later on, she made sure I wrote them down on a piece of paper. Paper was a thing

139

treasured in the camp, but Rachel explained to my mother that she liked my poems. Besides that, they would be very useful in many respects. First, the poems provided me with a mental occupation; other than Rafik, I had nobody to talk with. In addition, the poems would help me practice my writing. I had only finished the third grade in the ghetto, and was still writing poorly. Finally, they could serve as an important testament to the times.

My mother brought me a notebook and a pencil from the storehouse. Each evening I was happy to write down the poem I had made during the course of the day at work. Rachel corrected my poems, and so my spelling improved.

On the last day of the year we were again taken to the showers, but this time it was different. After months we finally were able to wash ourselves with warm water. We got soap and a clean towel. The clothes we had taken off before showering were quickly returned to us. They had been disinfected, and stank of chemicals.

On New Year's Eve, 1943, we received a double ration of bread. A good atmosphere prevailed in the camp; there were even signs of joy. The lights were turned off later that evening; from outside we could hear the celebratory gunshots of the Germans, happy shouts, and the voices of those who were drunk.

Later we sang quietly. As always, I sang for the women: songs of Vilnius; songs from the ghetto, and also partisan songs; the song about Wittenberg, for example. Something like hope began to grow in the women's hearts: hope that the war would come to an end and that we would be free; hope that we could go back home to Vilnius and perhaps find our loved ones waiting there. Later I lay with open eyes and thought over a poem. I wanted to write it down the next day, when I had a free moment.

Thus I found a wonderful way to fly far away, into a

world that was good, into a world of dreams and good fortune.

The new year brought new worries, sicknesses, cold, and hunger. Transportees arrived once again—Russian prisoners of war. When we saw them, we knew their imprisonment had been substantially worse than ours. They were tired and ill. Their clothes were in rags. Most of them had frostbite and frozen feet, ears, and noses. The men were so starved that they were ready to eat the soles of their shoes. This shocked us so greatly that, despite our miserable situation, we began to let them have some of our food. But it wasn't long before the prisoners of war were taken somewhere else; where, we never found out.

From time to time, at irregular intervals, "actions" took place in our women's camp. Gradually, we began to foresee when an "action" was about to take place. The Germans began to display a certain tenseness, and their shouting and abuse grew louder.

One day my mother ordered me to join a work crew that did construction work far away from the camp. I opposed her, as had been happening more and more often recently. But I had no choice this time, and I left the camp with the crew of women. Rachel Krinski and Dascha had been working on this crew for a long time. The evening before, I had heard my mother tell them that the officer in the clothing depot had become very nervous. He had drunk a great deal of schnapps, and talked over and over, meaningfully, of "tomorrow."

At the outdoor construction site, it was cold and I was shivering all over. Latvian civilian workers were also working there. They spoke halting Russian, but the women from Vilnius understood them. The civilians were local construction workers and skilled workers. We prisoners had to carry out the filthy auxiliary jobs. We passed cold bricks in brigades, carried bags of limestone to upper floors, and things like that.

There was almost no interchange between the women and the Letts—conversation was forbidden; but I picked up on glances now and then that said more than words. At times Rachel brought the Letts something or other from our camp—a piece of clothing, gloves, sometimes a piece of jewelry that she had gotten from my mother—in trade for bread. On occasion, Dascha got cigarettes. They brought back the food to camp—to my mother and the other women.

So the women succeeded in managing under extremely hard circumstances. From the workers they also heard news about what was going on in the world—especially the German-Russian front. That way we learned about the victories of the Russian army and their advances; and about the partisan fighting in the forests around Riga. Sometimes we even got greetings from the A.E.G. camp, the big electrical industry factory. Now and then we also got news of Dolka.

The day on the construction site was very difficult for me. My hands got chapped and cracked; my body hurt. In the evening we climbed, tired, into the truck that was to take us back to camp. A nervous atmosphere prevailed. We were all hoping we would find the others healthy and whole in the camp.

We arrived and climbed down from the truck. In the blockhouse there were fewer women than before. The silence was tense. I tried to find my mother, and at first I couldn't. Rachel took me by the hand and helped me look. We finally found my mother at the toilet.

She was standing, bent over the bowl, and vomiting. She seemed unable to stop. At once someone ran to the sick barracks and Dr. Bolek arrived. He laid my mother down on her bed and tried to talk with her, calm her, and give her water. She was completely worn out from the ceaseless vomiting. Slowly she became quieter. When it was time for lights-out and Dr. Bolek had to leave the women's camp, he sent one of the young women doctors who was working with him to my mother. Frau Dr. Resnik stayed with my mother the whole night. I climbed down to sleep in the lower bunk. I didn't ask questions; no one said anything to me; the blockhouse was quiet. Was I aware there was emptiness around me, and that I was lying alone in Niussia's and Rafik's bed? I don't know; I was tired and immediately fell asleep. The next morning, after roll call, I went back to the battery factory with my usual work crew. No one held me back.

My mother did only what was absolutely necessary. She tied the cloths about my head; she gave me the piece of bread for breakfast. But she said no word; she didn't cry; it was as if she were made of stone.

That same day, after I had returned to the blockhouse from work, I climbed up on Rachel's bunk and sat down next to her. I was alone again, and didn't know what I should do. What had happened? Nobody would tell me. My mother was acting as if she weren't there, as if she didn't even see me.

Only after a few days, when the first shock had worn off, did my mother pull herself together. She began to care for me more attentively, hugging me again and again and trying to get close to me. Then, suddenly, she broke her silence and told me everything.

On the day we all left the camp, and only those working in camp had remained behind, trucks had pulled up. The Germans went into the sick barracks the first thing, and began to take out the sick, one at a time. Some of the ill were carried on stretchers; others were supported by doctors or nurses.

Dr. Bolek tried to rescue every single one, and to convince the Germans that most of them were only slightly ill, not truly sick. He encouraged the sick to smile, get out of bed, and stand on their own feet. He dressed them in the clothes the attendants brought, but without success. The sick barracks was cleaned out, and only one or two people succeeded in escaping.

The doctors gave the sick people a few of the medicines they had available in order to calm them before they were taken away. But that was a waste, for these wouldn't be of any use to them anymore. The few medicines there were should actually have been saved for those who might be sick in the future, who could perhaps be saved.

The Germans then spread out over the Jewish men's camp and took everyone still remaining there. The men tried to escape, but the Germans released their dogs. These hunted down the men with loud baying. The poor wretches went running back and forth until they were nabbed by their pursuers and taken to the trucks.

Niussia and my mother were in the clothing depot all this time. Both of them were terribly worried about Rafik. My mother tried to convince her friend to leave Rafik in his hiding place in the blockhouse, between the headboard of the bunk and the wall. But Niussia wouldn't be calmed. After a while, when the barking dogs could be heard, she decided to fetch Rafik from his hiding place and bring him to the clothing depot. She would hide him among the clothes for one or two days. My mother declared herself ready to help her. They took a hamper, filled it up with blankets and pillows, and went into the camp.

A guard whom both of them knew well stood at the gate to the women's camp. He was a Ukrainian from the Vlassov district, which had sold out the Soviet army and gone over to the German side at the beginning of the war. Some of them were now serving as guards at the camp gates. Most were anti-Semites. They liked standing guard and giving orders, and being intoxicated by their power. This specific guard, however, was one of the "good" ones. From time to time he directed a few words in his Russian mother tongue at the women who passed by him. Therefore, with no misgivings, the two women went straight to Blockhouse 2, in which we were living.

The hamper they were carrying was a type of wooden box carried between two poles, like a stretcher. Niussia laid Rafik in this hamper and covered him with pillows and blankets. My mother stood guard while Niussia was preparing the hamper. Then they picked it up and set off for the gate. My mother went in front, and Niussia behind; the hamper was between them. It was only when they reached the gate that they noticed that another guard now stood there, a man notorious for his cruelty. The two women walked on without hesitating. The guard stopped them and asked them what they were carrying. They answered that they had been sent to fetch blankets for disinfection. The guard was suspicious; perhaps he was only showing off in front of the two women. At any rate, he began to jab at the hamper with the tip of his bayonet, and he hit Rafik. The boy cried out and was immediately discovered. All three of them were grabbed and beaten.

In the clothing depot the news spread like lightning. Hans, the officer responsible for the clothing depot, immediately came running and swore that he had sent the two women into the camp to collect the blankets. In order to save my mother, Niussia said she had concealed Rafik without my mother's knowledge. The officer succeeded in freeing my mother after a short time. Then he tried every trick in the book to obtain a written release order for Niussia from the camp commandant. He succeeded, too. At once he ran back to the courtyard of the camp to the spot where the trucks were being loaded with people. Niussia and Rafik and some other women were standing together and waiting for the next truck. Hans turned to the officer in charge and showed him the written directive. Then he went to Niussia, pulled her by the arm, and tried to persuade her to stay. But Niussia wouldn't let go of Rafik's hand. When everyone was being loaded onto the truck, the guard came to take Rafik, and Niussia went with her son, quietly and resolutely. Together, hand in hand, they climbed into the truck.

Hans was still trying to persuade Niussia to stay; he said that her son hadn't much longer to live, anyway. But Niussia, who was already standing in the truck, said loudly and firmly, in purest German, "It is worth sacrificing my whole life, so that my son can feel safe and at peace for half an hour."

The truck began to move. Through the window of the clothing depot, my mother saw the face of her friend as she stood on the tailgate.

Those were Niussia's last words. About two hours later Hans returned to the clothing depot. He came in, slammed the door shut with his foot, and screamed loudly, "Niussia is no more!" So we understood that she had been executed.

He had bottles of schnapps with him, and he locked himself up in his room.

After a few hours, when he was completely drunk, and the women were afraid of him, he came out of his room like a wounded animal. With powerful gestures, he pushed over all the shelves that stood in his path. Glass, valuables, and everything else went flying helter-skelter. Finally, he collapsed on a heap of clothes and fell asleep.

PRISONER NUMBER 5083:
SUSIE WEKSLER

TIME PASSED. In the battery factory where I was working, the atmosphere had changed greatly. The mood was quiet and sad. Most of the women working there were Jewish women from Germany; we called them "the Deutschers." In the past years they had gone through a lot, and here in Kaiserwald they were managing pretty well. They held a high position within the camp. To begin with, they spoke German and found it easy to communicate with the guards. Secondly, among the guard detail or the political prisoners, they sometimes met someone from their hometown; someone who had perhaps lived on the same street, and with whom they were linked to a common past, common memories. And thirdly, most of them still had husbands, brothers, or sons on the other side of the fence, in the Jewish men's camp.

That was also the reason why some of them preferred to work in the factory, even though it was hard and dirty work and there was no possibility of "organizing" additional food there. But when they went through the narrow passage between the fences of the two men's camps, they could see their men and hear their voices.

The last "action" had struck the men's camp severely. Over half of the prisoners had been taken away, and many of our women had lost their loved ones.

Up to then we had hoped an "action" served only to transfer prisoners from one camp to another, but now we learned that—at least in the last one—the people had been sent to their death. Until now we had thought that the railway cars running past to the forest on the narrow tracks next to the women's camp were used only for transporting work materials or foodstuffs to the camp, or bringing batteries to the factory. But now we heard there were also railway cars that took people to their death.

We had known for a long time that there were groups of partisans in the forests. From time to time we heard gunshots and saw movement among the trees. Now the partisans had succeeded in penetrating up to the battery factory. One day I was called outside. Mrs. Maier, our supervisor, said I should help carry the newly arrived batteries. I was surprised. Until then I had never had to do this heavy labor. But while I was working, a woman asked me in German, "Susie, do you know Russian?"

"Yes, I understand it pretty well, but I can hardly speak it."

"Behind the last pile of batteries is someone. He maintains he's a partisan; he has a weapon. You needn't fear him; he's come because he wants to tell us something. It seems to be important, and we don't understand him. Go to him. Mrs. Maier will keep watch. In case of danger, we'll give you a signal."

I was very afraid, but I had no time to reflect. I took a few batteries and went to the place they had told me about.

The man sitting behind the heap of batteries was dressed like a hunter and held a gun. He spoke halting Russian; to my own amazement, I noticed I was answering him in Polish. But we understood one another. He told me to let the women know that the partisans were close by and if anyone wanted to join them, it could be arranged. Besides that, he warned us that the Germans planned to kill all the prisoners in the camp.

I didn't understand this; after all, we were working, and anyone who had been taken from the camp had only been taken to another camp farther away. The partisan could see I was only a child and didn't understand the situation, for he said quietly, "Give the women the message that the last group from the men's camp, which left a few days ago, wasn't taken away to work. The men, and the few boys who were with them, were taken to the forest. There they were loaded into closed railway cars and asphyxiated with gas. Afterward the side doors of the railway cars were opened, the cars were jacked up, and the bodies were dumped into a big grave in the forest. The partisans saw it happen."

I was frightened and couldn't believe it. The short conversation was at an end, for the guard was approaching and I got a signal to go back to work. I did so, and the women immediately noticed how terrified and pale I was.

Mrs. Maier went with me to the toilet, as if we both had to relieve ourselves. We squatted down side by side, over the openings of the latrine, and I told her everything the partisan had said. Mrs. Maier grew pale and suddenly sank to the ground. She had understood the man better than I. I fetched help, then went back to my work.

The upset was so great that nobody could work further. Mrs. Maier's daughter, Helga, was crying. Only I stayed quiet; I was unable to express my feelings. That day, when we walked back between the two camps, one or two women said something in German to the men. The Jewish men and also the non-Jews immediately understood. It became quiet. We walked between the fences, and the dismal silence accompanied us.

In the blockhouse I had to tell everything again, over and over, until I was sick of it. It was decided to send some women who could speak good Russian to the factory the next day. After a few days we learned that women from the camp were missing. A few young women had decided to use the opportunity to flee to the partisans. When their escape was detected, a huge roll call was held for the entire camp. My mother was scared. She whispered to me that I should keep quiet and in no way draw attention to myself, for, after all, I was mixed up with the first meeting with the partisans.

We stood there many hours. Germans with dogs came, and shouted, but the missing women remained at large. After standing for hours, we got the "at ease" order and could go back into the blockhouses.

My mother was afraid to send me back to work in the factory, because someone might somehow figure out how the contact with the partisans had come about. She was also afraid of betrayal, and so the next day she sent me off with a group of women who cleaned the rooms of the commandant's office.

I didn't know what to do there. A woman took charge of me, and we cleaned the floor and the stairs and polished boots. When I came back from work, I told my mother that I didn't want to go there anymore. The many Germans in the commandant's office had frightened me. My mother promised she would ask the officer if I could work with her in the clothing depot from now on. He actually agreed.

I was almost happy there in the barracks. It was warm, and I got something extra to eat; I could wear normal clothes, and besides that, I wasn't really working. I sat there and played with the toys and dolls I found in the clothing depot.

I liked best the shelf with the dishes. There were colorful crystal glasses and painted glass; splendid china; and various small porcelain figures. I pretended I was a princess walking among her treasures, and that the high shelves were the streets of a big world without borders. While I was playing quietly, my mother suddenly burst in. With a deadly serious face, she pulled me to the back room and ordered me to climb between the clothes and the mattresses and keep quiet.

Silence. Suddenly the heavy tread of German soldiers was heard in the clothing depot. I heard people running, the noise of boots, strange voices, and a loud discussion at the door. My heart skipped a beat when I heard the key turning in the door lock, and Hans saying, "Nobody's here; these are clothes from the infirmary that are dirty and will have to be burned. A few cases of stomach typhus were diagnosed, and now an epidemic must be prevented. I can't let anyone into this room because of the danger of contagion."

The steps went away, and quiet prevailed again. I felt drained and empty, and I was unable to stop trembling.

In the evening my mother fetched me from the hiding place, and together we went back to the camp. Here we learned that a "punishment action" had taken place because of the escapees; again most of the people in the infirmary had been taken away. They had also taken any weak women who had remained in the blockhouses that day.

The officer wouldn't let my mother take me to work in the clothing depot anymore. So I went back to the battery factory. The smallest pieces of batteries came to my table. They looked like small tin pipes, filled with tamped-down carbon. In the middle was the anode, a small, encased rod with a metal head. I had to pry the tin away from the rod; I did this by laying a knife along the little pipe and hitting it with a hammer. I widened the opening with the knife. Out of the tiny pipe came an acid in the form of a gooey yellow paste, and a little cloth sack filled with the carbon. The little sack was smeared with yellow, stinking goo that irritated the skin. I had to remove that goo with the knife and collect it in a container provided for it. Then I opened the little sack, took out the carbon, and tossed it into a box for carbon, which stood in front of me. Now the anode rod was free, and I laid it in the carton reserved for it. I threw the dirty, sticky little sack into the trash bin.

The work wasn't hard, but it was wearisome. You had to

work quickly, and the paste burned your hands. If you got it on your face, it left a red mark behind, as if you had burned yourself. Fine dust always swirled out when I took the carbon out of the little sack. I was breathing carbon dust the whole day; I felt as if my lungs were full of dust. The women all had carbon-dust-blackened skin, and their hands were covered with caustic wounds. Washing didn't help.

The atmosphere in the factory was pleasant. The women were quiet and followed the instructions of the supervisor. They didn't fight with each other. On the contrary, they helped one another to lift the heavy batteries, carry the full boxes of carbon, and dismantle the batteries. When a woman was suffering from especially bad caustic burns on her hands, the others would try to take over her work and give her a break from contact with the acid. To please our supervisor, Genoveva Maier, one of the women had written a song for her; we sang it on the way to work.

We worked quickly, in order to finish our daily quota. Until the quota had been met, we couldn't leave. The materials we recovered were then packed up and sent to various factories outside the camp.

The sergeant in charge avoided frequent contact with the German army, the branch of the armed forces to which he belonged. And he behaved relatively humanely. He was small, quiet, and earnest—a gray, unassuming man whom you might meet anywhere. He had been drafted by the army, and was glad when he got assigned to the factory, far away from the front, far away from the war. He had left a wife and a daughter, Susanne, back home in Hannover. He called me Susanne, too, and I often noticed he was looking at me.

I was scared of him, despite the impression he gave of quietness and trustworthiness. I worried he might discover my secret—that I was just eleven years old. For that reason, I tried to not be near him very often.

In this way, a couple of months passed. Again and again, recently, women were taken from the camp. There was an "action" almost every day, and more and more bunks were empty in the blockhouses. It looked as though they wanted to make room for newcomers.

One day a truck appeared, and soldiers sprang out; but this time it happened at my workplace, the battery factory. We recognized the signal and were crippled with fear.

The sergeant, too, saw what was coming. He was sitting in his room, way at the back of the barracks. When he heard the noise, he came into the workroom. That day I was sitting at the far end of the table, next to the door of his room. He came to me and grabbed me firmly by my arm. I was deathly afraid, and tried to free myself from his grasp. He saw my fear, but he gripped me tightly, gave me a smack, and shoved me into his room. He followed me in. Quickly opening a coal bin that stood next to the iron stove, he ordered me to get into it. Crazed and fearful, I did what he said. He pushed me even deeper inside, then closed the lid over me with a bang.

It was dark in the box, and the little air there was, was full of coal dust. Rigid with terror, I realized that the sergeant wanted to protect me. Only now did it become clear to me that he knew I was a child; and here I had been thinking I was acting like an adult.

Germans came into the room for a minute—a minute that seemed like an eternity to me. Farther off, I heard cries and the sound of blows; then it was quiet. I lay in the coal bin and couldn't move. The sharp edges of the coal pressed in on me from all sides. I was unable to turn over or change my position even a little. The smell was terrible and I was breathing black dust. I lay there a long time, unable to think; unable to cry.

When the sergeant raised the lid, it was already dark outside. There was no one else besides him in the barracks. He calmed me, gave me bread to eat, and explained that it would be better for me to stay there, in the factory, over-night. I tried to say that my mother would worry, but he cut me off. "It's all right. Mrs. Maier knows all about it."

That night I stayed alone in the factory, far away from the other people. I lay down on the lid of the coal bin in the sergeant's room. The stove was no longer burning, and I had neither a blanket nor anything else with which to cover my-self. Besides that, the electricity had been turned off, and I could see nothing. When my eyes had adjusted to the dark-ness a little, I decided to go to the toilet. Finally, after a long time, I was once again alone when I went to the bathroom. That seemed so wonderful to me that all the difficulties of the night seemed insignificant.

The next morning other women came with the work crew. They took the places of those who had been taken away the previous day. At the end of work, when I came back to the camp with the crew, my mother was waiting for me. She hugged and kissed me, and we both knew we had succeeded—with a lot of luck—in once again surviving a se-lection and staying alive.

It was the end of February or the beginning of March. One morning we stood yet again on the roll call ground. This time the roll call took especially long. It was cold and wet. The blitz maidens checked the blockhouses, counting and tallying the numbers, and we stood outside. A fine, dense rain had already been falling for days, and the surface of the roll call ground had turned to mire. We stood still; high-ranking officers appeared. Inspection. Here and there women began to waver; it was hard for them to stand still so many hours. We were tired and hungry and stiff from the cold; our clothes were wet and the rain was lashing at us. After six hours' standing outside, when the "at ease" order came, and the kettle with breakfast had been brought to its place, my mother collapsed and fell down into the mud.

Immediately, helping hands were extended. Women lifted her up, stood her on her feet, and supported her while she leaned on one of the women, so as not to attract the attention of the Germans who hadn't yet left the camp. The officers moved off without having noticed us. I pushed through to my mother's side and saw that her eyes were closed. The women carried her to the infirmary.

She hadn't been feeling well for a long time, since the day when Niussia and Rafik had gone from us. It had begun with vomiting and stomach pains, the same as last time, after the separation from Dolka. Everything my mother put into her mouth she vomited back up; so she had stopped eating and gave me her ration. Because I was always hungry, I hadn't noticed that my mother ate nothing anymore. She became weaker and weaker; her condition worsened after every "action." She had diarrhea, and it was hard for her to stand at roll call, because she so often had to run to the toilet. Sometimes she went to Dr. Bolek and got sedatives from him, but they didn't help. Once or twice her friends "organized" a fresh potato for her; although any one of us would have gladly eaten it, we burned it. The charcoal might help alleviate my mother's terrible diarrhea. But nothing had worked. Now she had broken down. The hardest part of my life began on that day. I was left alone.

After my mother had been admitted to the sick barracks, Dr. Bolek called me to him and spoke seriously with me. He made me swear to stick to my daily routine: to get up first; to dress myself and put myself to rights; to go to work in the factory; to divide my bread into two portions in the evening, so that I should still have something in the morning; and—

especially—to visit my mother twice a day, before roll call and in the evening after work. Dr. Bolek said my presence would be very important; only thus could he rescue my mother.

When I visited her in the first days, my mother wasn't aware of me at all. I sat next to her, holding her hand, but she didn't react. She had been taken to the rearmost room of the barracks. It was the Dying Room—strictly speaking, the room for anyone receiving no further medicine, because that would only mean "wasting" it. But Dr. Bolek didn't forget how my mother had helped him in procuring medicines. For that reason he was trying everything, and giving her what medicines he had at his disposal.

I moved among the women in the blockhouse as if I weren't there. The women were tired and concerned with their own problems; they hardly noticed me.

Each morning I got up early, as I had promised, but I didn't succeed in binding the turban and headscarf properly. Mrs. Maier noticed it and helped me put it right.

I was working hard, but Karola, the blockhouse kapo, rarely remembered to give me an extra plate of soup. I bolted the first plate of soup that I got, but didn't succeed in pushing my way through the women to the kettle in order to get seconds. The fight over the kettle was extremely tough. When the kettle was empty, women would climb inside it and try to lick out the last drops of soup with their tongues and hands.

In the evenings, when I came back to the blockhouse, I went into the washroom. But with the crowd about the faucets, the cold water, and the skimpy piece of soap I had, I could hardly wash off the top layer of black dust that stuck to my body. I couldn't wash my clothes properly, either, and I wasn't strong enough to wring all the water out of them. My underpants and shirt were still very wet in the morning.

I was alone; no one bothered about me. And although I

was already grown up in my own eyes, I had no one to counsel me. Rachel, who slept next to me on the bunk, encouraged me and sometimes tried to help me, but her work was hard and she was at the end of her own strength. Earlier she and her friends had been able to "organize" additional food with the help of the exchangeable things my mother had brought with her from the clothing depot. But that was all over now, and they too were suffering badly from hunger. I suffered especially. In the first couple of weeks of my mother's illness, I still found dry bread in our hiding place; but each day the supply dwindled, and one day it was gone.

Now the period of great hunger began. All our additional food was exhausted. Hunger tormented me so greatly, I couldn't think anymore. I went through all the motions to which I had become accustomed during our months in the camp, but it was just automatic. Because of the hunger, I slept badly; I hallucinated, had bad dreams, and woke up because I had been screaming and crying in my sleep. I hallucinated when I was awake, too; terrors pursued me.

At work I couldn't concentrate. I sat there daydreaming by the hour. Because of that, I was constantly wounding myself with the knife, and on the sharp tin; the wounds on my hands became filthy from the burning yellow paste. I no longer made poems, and had also stopped singing.

I looked terrible. I found walking so difficult that I only shuffled. Dirt clung to me; I had become thin and was only a shadow of myself. Even the turban didn't improve my appearance. It was filthy and sat on my head, skewed and messy. An eerie indifference had taken hold of me.

One day, small, shrunken, and dirty, I went to visit my mother. I was shivering from the cold, and had wrapped myself in the blanket I had taken from my bed. After almost two months with no response, I suddenly found her in full possession of her senses. When she became aware of how I was looking, behaving, and walking, she cried, "Mussulman!" "Mussulmen" was the word for those who had lost hope, stopped fighting, and were waiting indifferently for their end. Mussulmen lay down in the corners of the squares or blockhouses, gradually lost their senses, and died.

Throughout our time in the ghetto and in the camp, my mother had always said that you couldn't neglect yourself, that you had to fight and always believe that one day the troubles would pass. If you gave up, it was a waste of all the trouble you had already endured. You had to look after your appearance, and must not become a Mussulman. I was therefore startled to hear her call me by that name; I also heard the reproach in her voice. All of a sudden I understood that something bad had happened to me. At once I shed the blanket—the first sign of a Mussulman—and straightened up. My mother smiled, and her smile seemed to me as though the sun were shining again. I knew she was doing better, that the worst was over, and that there was now hope she would get well again. Dr. Bolek also observed that my mother's condition had improved.

I don't know who helped whom more that day. It must have been that my wretched condition woke up my mother, and that her return to life also motivated my strength of will. I guess we helped each other reciprocally. It would still take a long time until we had both recovered, however.

Dr. Bolek told me to come and be checked out at the infirmary barracks. He couldn't believe his eyes. I was filthy. My whole body was covered with red spots; I scratched myself constantly and was terribly infested with lice. My hands were covered with wounds and were festering. My lips were also cracked and covered with running sores. I could eat solid food only with difficulty, because my mouth hurt so much. Dr. Bolek decided to keep me at the sick barracks for a few days.

This was very dangerous for me. Dr. Bolek had all he

could do to protect my mother from the "actions" that broke over the sick barracks. Once a week there was an "examination" of the sick. The German doctors didn't really examine the sick people. They only checked the lists to see how long they had stayed in the sick barracks, what illnesses they suffered from, and so on. If they discovered that someone had been sick for longer than a week, he was "evacuated," which meant he was ordered taken away.

That's why Dr. Bolek, along with Frau Dr. Resnik, was hiding my mother. Each week they changed her name on the list and moved her from one bed to another. From the moment she could leave her bed even for a short time, she was certified as being strong enough to work.

And then typhoid broke out in the camp. The women who were sick with typhoid lay in a closed room, separated from the others. After a two-day stay in the sick barracks, they were "evacuated." Dr. Bolek suffered under these terrible conditions. He tried to hide those poor sick people who landed in the sick barracks—dirty, stinking, crawling with lice, senseless, and with diarrhea.

The doctors and the nurses were disgusted by them, but Dr. Bolek braced himself and treated them, washed them, cleaned them, and examined them. Because of the threat of contagion, another, smaller building was erected next to the sick barracks. In this building clothes could be washed and disinfected immediately.

Dr. Bolek placed me in the hands of Frau Dr. Resnik. She personally took it on herself to make sure I washed myself properly with very hot water. This freed me from the dirt of two months, from the carbon, from the burning paste, from the sores and the lice. My clothes were disinfected and washed in hot water.

This was the third time since my arrival at the camp that I was able to wash myself with hot water. Afterward Frau Dr. Resnik cleaned my wounds. She bandaged them after applying a soothing and healing salve to them. I got enough to eat in the sick barracks. I didn't know where the extra bread and the extra rations of soup came from, but I didn't ask. I ate and enjoyed the food. As I moved among the sick people and sat long hours by my mother's side, I learned that the extra rations had belonged to those who had died, and whose names hadn't yet been reported.

My mother told me a lot about the other sick people there. Among all the sad stories, there was also sometimes a funny one. A young woman lay next to my mother. She wasn't really sick; she was weak and didn't know what was going on around her. Every night she peed in her bed, although she was capable of getting up and going to the toilet. In the morning, when she was asked why she had peed in her bed, she said, "I was so cold, and wanted to warm myself a bit." We had to laugh about it.

In all sorrows there are also good moments. Dr. Bolek continued to pass his medical expertise on to Frau Dr. Resnik. The young woman, who had finished her education shortly before the beginning of the war, had surely imagined that her first professional experience would be something completely different. Now she was getting a further education here, in hell. It was hard for the young, sensitive woman to bear all that filth, the severe illnesses, the abscesses, the many wounds that wouldn't heal, the sick people who looked more dead than alive, and whom she was unable to help. The feeling of helplessness tormented her, but Dr. Bolek fought on. Out of their common work, and the high esteem she had for that likable man, there grew love—a tender love without hope. Dr. Bolek was always at her side, helping her and performing the dirty work in her place. For her he was the superior, the teacher, the brother, and at the same time also true friend and beloved.

The typhoid spread further. The German doctor in charge decided to order all the women in the sick barracks and in the entire camp examined. The doctors and nurses looked at blood and stools. It came to light that two young women—sisters—were the pathogenic carriers of the typhoid. The two pretty young women, twenty and twenty-two years old, were isolated in a new shed next to the sick barracks; there they waited for their death.

Each day I passed by this shed and looked in to see if the two—condemned to death—were still there. All the women worried about them.

In the morning, when we went to the roll call ground, we went by the fence and looked in the window; a weight fell from our hearts if they were still there. It was the same in the evenings. Another day had passed. They were still alive.

One day, when I returned from work and went to the sick barracks to visit my mother, the window of the new shed stood open, and I suddenly knew their suffering was at an end. They had taken them away to be killed.

After I had been released from the sick barracks and had gone back to my work in the factory, I again suffered from hunger. But at least my mother was getting stronger and stronger. Her acquaintances came to visit her now, and sometimes she asked me to bring this or that woman to her. One day Mascha and Batja Efron visited my mother. They were two sisters who slept on the bunk opposite me. Afterward my mother ordered me to give them one of the two pieces of soap that contained the rings. We had held on to them from the first shower.

After two days I got bread from Batja; from then on I received a few extra slices every few days. I divided them carefully, so they would last longer. I asked the two sisters where the bread came from, because now I wanted to know and understand everything going on about me. After they had conversed with one another, they told me they were in touch with civilian Letts at their workplace. They had succeeded in finding a man who was prepared to deliver bread for a few weeks, in exchange for my mother's valuable ring. They brought the bread into the camp and divided it between themselves and me. Once again a piece of family jewelry had extended my life for a few weeks.

In April of 1944 a new shipment of women arrived in the camp; a big and very sad shipment. It was comprised of Jewish women from Hungary. They came directly from Auschwitz to Kaiserwald. Thus we came to learn of that horrendous camp. Until then we hadn't known where other camps were located, and we had heard absolutely nothing yet about extermination camps like Auschwitz. In work camps like ours, people were killed, it's true; but we didn't yet know about crematoria and gas chambers.

The young women were completely terrified when they arrived. Only a short while before they had been living with their families in their own homes in Hungary—in villages and provincial capitals. Then, one day, they had suddenly been assembled together and deported to Auschwitz. There they had been separated from their families. Everything had been taken from them; their heads had been shaved bald; a number had been tattooed on their arms; and they had been dressed in striped prisoner's clothing.

They were young, between eighteen and twenty-five years old, terrified, and crazed. Everything that we long-term inmates had survived in the course of two or three years, they had had happen to them within a month or two. They walked about with gray faces and shorn heads on which the hair was already beginning to grow back. Their big, black eyes held the look of hunted animals. They wore thin, striped clothes, torn, and without jackets. Through the big holes, the gray skin of their bodies could be seen. Their narrow shoulders were bent, their breasts shrunken. They looked more like ugly birds than people.

We old hands pitied the poor girls and helped them, as far as it was possible. But the Hungarian women lost their will to live. Soon most of them changed into Mussulmen. They didn't try to go to work. They stood about the blockhouses, leaning on the walls and staring into the air. Indifference, hunger, and sickness were the reasons that many of them died, even in the first days after their arrival.

In order to make room for the Hungarians in the blockhouses, we were now sleeping four to a bunk once more. Batja and Mascha Efron took me into theirs. It was fortunate I had once again started to wash and was clean, so they could stand having me next to them. Even so, I continued to hit out in my sleep.

In the evenings we talked sometimes. Both of them had been teachers, and Batja promised to teach me a little. During my stay here, I had learned to speak German, and could even sing a couple of German songs. I had picked them up at work. The women from Germany were knowledgeable about German culture, and sometimes they sang songs or declaimed classic German poetry. I paid attention and learned. So I came to know Heine's "Lorelei," for instance. It was a song forbidden in Nazi Germany because, to the Nazis, Heine—despite his baptism—had remained a Jew. Now Batja wanted to acquaint me with the history of the people of Israel; each evening she told me an installment. I took pleasure in the beautiful sayings and stories that widened my narrow, small world.

Each day toward evening, when I came back to our blockhouse from the infirmary barracks, it was almost dark outside already. One evening I saw a shadow next to our blockhouse. I was terrified. Hardly anyone was outside at this time of day. After the distribution of food, most women remained in the blockhouses; they sat at the long table, or on their bunks. They slowly ate the meager bread, chewing thoroughly to keep the bread in their mouths as long as possible. It was more satisfying that way, and one had the taste of it longer.

Carefully and quietly I crept closer, for I had to pass the shadow in order to get into the blockhouse. Suddenly I stopped, as if frozen. My mouth opened, but no sound came out. Against the blockhouse wall stood Dascha. Over her was bent a man, a kapo—a German with a black chevron, a criminal. He was squeezing her with all his strength, and she was letting out sounds that sounded like crying to me. The whole thing seemed horribly awful and brutal to me.

I glided by them. They didn't see me at all. I didn't know what I should do. I wanted to help Dascha, but didn't know how. Terrified, my teeth chattering with fear, I raced into the blockhouse, to Rachel Krinski, and tearfully begged her to help Dascha. Rachel asked what was wrong, and when I told her what I had seen, she comforted me and told me that Dascha would surely soon return and that I shouldn't worry about it. I didn't understand Rachel's lack of concern; after all, they were friends. Why was she so calm? Was she afraid to help Dascha?

After a short time Dascha came into the blockhouse. She was calm, as though nothing had happened. She climbed up onto her bunk and lit a cigarette. One of the women sitting on the beds said, "You've got cigarettes again," and Dascha nodded.

That night it was hard for me to fall asleep. Over and over the scene played out before my eyes, but I shrank from saying or asking anything. It was one more secret that the women wouldn't explain to me. In the following days I secretly watched Dascha off and on, but I couldn't detect anything unusual about her.

Finally, my mother came back to our blockhouse—after a stay of one hundred days in the sick barracks. It was exactly one hundred days; she had counted them herself.

From now on, when she became sick, she always said it would last one hundred days; she couldn't get well any faster.

She was weak and pale, and her hair, which had grown back a bit in the interval, was completely white. She took care of me again, and made sure I was washing myself. She went back to work at her former place—in the clothing depot. I was glad, because she brought me new underpants and a new undershirt, and also a new headscarf.

Spring had arrived. It was warmer, and in the evenings, we stayed outside on the grounds until it became dark. On especially warm evenings we sometimes sat in a circle and sang quietly. The men stood at the fence of their camp and listened to us. They asked for me to sing, and I was happy to.

May, you remind us of freedom,
and awaken longing
for everything that's gone. . . .

It was a song that doubtless sprang up in the ghetto. At least, that is where I first heard it. I also sang Russian songs translated into Yiddish. Anyone who knew the songs sang along. The singing woke hope in the hearts of the women.

When the summer arrived, I found additional nourishment in the forest about the battery factory: blueberries. They grew not only in the woods, but also between the heaps of batteries. Besides the berries, I also found thick, sour-tasting stalks. The women in the factory called them rhubarb. We dug out the stalks with our hands and sucked on them, and the acidity puckered our mouths. But we were so hungry, we ate everything. We sucked a long time on the stalks, and it turned out that they were a good thing, and were helping to get rid of the sores on our lips.

So passed the spring and the summer of the year 1944.

I was making poems again, and writing them in my

notebook. I already had two notebooks full, and Rachel Krinski corrected my writing style and encouraged me to continue.

Because I had no one to talk with, I often withdrew into myself and dreamed. I constructed a fantasy world for myself and spent hours lost in it. There I was happy and free. A happy girl at home, who ate bread with butter and jam to her heart's content; who spooned up good, hot soup, and drank milk. White bread and milk were the most tempting things I could imagine. I dreamed of a hot, perfumed bath, and afterward a white, soft bed in which to sleep; alone, like a princess. But I always woke up and had to return to the terrible reality.

The Jewish high holy days, Rosh Hashanah and Yom Kippur of 1944, were approaching, and with them, the autumn, with its rain and our fear of the cold. One day we sensed something was in the wind. That morning, at roll call, the tension was widespread. After roll call my mother shoved me toward a work crew that was riding to a construction site far from the camp. I tried to rejoin my own crew, but my mother threw me a warning glance; I gave in and climbed with the other women into the truck that was to take us to work.

There I worked on the cement mixer. The women showed me what I had to do: bring water, dump it into the machine, empty sacks of cement into the machine. The cement was terribly dusty, and I coughed the whole time, but now, at least, I was only gray-white and not black from carbon.

Most of the women working there were from the group of Hungarian women. It came to me suddenly that they were behaving oddly. During work I heard them murmuring in their strange and—to me—incomprehensible language. The women about me moaned and groaned, raging at God, whispering among themselves, and raising their eyes to heaven. I had never seen anything like it. Astonished, I observed what was going on about me.

It was noon. Because the worksite was far away from the camp, we didn't go back there for our lunch break. All the women sat down on boards and rocks, and the pot with the soup was brought. The kapo began distributing it.

The women didn't stand up to receive their food. Strange. I sprang up at once, although I was tired, and got my soup. Slowly the other women came and got their portions. It was a very special soup, a thick and tasty bean soup in which large pieces of bacon and pork swam. It was hot and good—a meal fit for a king.

I ate it all up and licked my plate. I was happy. I didn't understand why the other women in the camp didn't know about this worksite. Only when I had finished eating did I realize that most of the women hadn't touched their soup. One after another they brought me their rations. I ate four or five helpings of soup and regretted that I was forced to stop when the lunch break was over and we had to go back to work.

Of course, many of the women were so exhausted that they could hardly work. When I wanted to know the reason why, it was explained to me they were hungry and therefore very tired. Astonished, I asked why they hadn't eaten their own soup themselves. They said that today was Yom Kippur. Normally, the meals here weren't so good, but it figured that on a day when Jews fasted, the women would be given thick, good soup. I decided to divide my bread that evening with the women who had given me their soup. We returned to camp, and—once again—the blockhouses had become emptier. This was the "Yom Kippur action," one of the final actions in Kaiserwald, although we didn't know it at the time.

In the following days several groups from other nearby work camps came to Kaiserwald: women from the A.B.A., the warehouse for German army uniforms, and from the factories of the A.E.G. and other companies. The camp filled up, and we had to sleep four to a bunk once more. Dolka came back to Kaiserwald, too, and my mother was relieved that she was alive. At least one of the worries plaguing her was now lifted from her. I was very glad about the reunion. Dolka was very thin and famished, and we shared our little food with her.

Genia was not among those who returned. We heard she had become sick at some point and had been taken away, but she hadn't returned to us. She had probably been taken directly to the railway cars for gassing.

Along with the women who came from outside, news also reached us of the victories of the Red Army and the approach of the front. Day by day we pictured the end of the war and the liberation.

The bombing of nearby Riga began, and from time to time, when the sirens were wailing and darkness covered the camp, we went outside into the square and looked up at the skies; maybe a bomb would drop on the camp. We longed for the day.

And then it came to this: The camp leadership and the Gestapo officers of Riga were looking for a way to flee the city and get away from the front, in order to save their skins. The evacuation was starting.

To begin with, the badges on our clothing were altered. Until then Jews wore the yellow star with their number; now we got a yellow triangle with the tip facing down, and above it a horizontal black stripe. That differentiated us from the other prisoners, but at the same time obscured the fact that we were Jewish. We supposed that we would be taken to Germany, to the "Reich." Because many of the areas of the Reich had been officially declared "free of Jews," our origin had to be kept secret from the local populations.

These suspicions spread among "the Deutsch-ers" and

made them glad. "Finally, back to the homeland," they said—and, so saying, inspired our resentment.

The Jewish women from Germany were hoping for better conditions in the "old homeland." But, as it would soon be clear, this hope was also in vain.

GÓWNO

RACHEL SAID, "You see, Susie? Everything comes to an end. Now things will begin to go our way; the Kaiserwald chapter is finished."

Yes, we were sure they would take us away from here; but we didn't know to where.

But people always hope for better times. After all we had suffered from hunger and cold, from beatings and hard labor, and especially from the many "actions," it was difficult for us to imagine something worse. For that reason we said, "Anything that comes along will have to be better." We knew the Russian army was very close; had we not been taken away from there, the Red Army would soon have freed us.

It was the last week of September. We had heard from the kapos and supervisors that we would set out on this day. So we took everything we had with us to roll call; perhaps a miracle would occur and the Red Army would arrive sooner? My mother took the piece of soap with the last ring from its hiding place. We put on double clothing, and my mother concealed the couple of slices of bread that remained to us under her dress, between the two pairs of panties she was wearing. Between my underpants I hid the two notebooks with my poems. I had wrapped them up in the warm headscarf I still possessed from last winter. And so we went to roll call.

Outside it was still dark. We stood on the roll call ground, and then the counting began. Once again it was an especially long roll call. The blockhouse commanders counted and checked the lists of the women over and over and went back and forth again and again between the blockhouses and the roll call ground. Roll calls were taking place in the entire camp: the men's camp; the women's camp; the transit camp. Even the infirmary was lined up for the last roll call.

After the painstaking count, the sick were allowed to go back to their barracks, but the doctors and nurses were kept in rows alongside the men and women of the camp.

After a few hours motorcycles and cars appeared. Black limousines, in which high-ranking officers dressed in black SS uniforms were sitting. Once again orders were given: "Quiet! Quiet!" The officers exchanged a few words with one another. Hungry and tired, we stood in the early-morning chill and feared what was to come.

Slowly it grew light. Blitz maidens and officers went from blockhouse to blockhouse and checked to see that no one remained there. They closed the windows of each blockhouse, then the doors, and the keys rattled in the locks. The blockhouse commanders and the kapos ran excitedly among the blockhouses. Then trucks arrived. The sick were loaded into them, as well as those who hadn't been in the sick barracks but the blockhouses, yet were incapable of going on foot. They were told that it was a special transport. And it truly was a "special transport" that received "special treatment." We never saw those unhappy people again.

All this took about five hours, and when the order to march out had been given, the sun stood high above our heads. It was a beautiful fall day. The forest sparkled in all its many colors, and the sun was shining. With conflicting feelings we left the place of our suffering.

The first groups to leave Kaiserwald came from the Jewish women's camp. We went in rank and file, reflecting the strict discipline we had become used to in a year.

We women from Vilnius had come here a year before, in October 1943. Many of those who had arrived with us were now missing. We went divided into five sections, five women to a row. At the head of the column, private black automobiles drove with their headlights on; ahead of and alongside us drove motorcycles. Besides these, we were surrounded by heavily armed guards. After about an hour we reached a small, deserted train station. We stopped and waited. To the sounds of loud yelling and the barking of dogs, the rows were straightened.

And then a train arrived: a locomotive with a few freight cars; and, behind them, a couple of completely empty passenger cars. The SS officers were the first to climb into these. The blitz maidens had a car, too. Well-dressed women and children civilians stepped out of the private automobiles. They climbed on board the train while soldiers carried their baggage and loaded it into one of the freight cars. My mother was looking from me to the children of the German officers. She was shaking her head and weeping.

After all the superior officers and their families were sitting in the train and ready to go, we got the order to climb aboard. All the prisoners had to push themselves into the few freight cars. Anyone who didn't succeed in squeezing in had to remain behind at the train station, and couldn't go. We understood what this meant. It meant that only those who made it onto the freight cars would stay alive. Anyone remaining would die here, on the railway platform. My mother whispered, "Right now we'll save our bones; someday we'll have some flesh to put on them."

All the women were now running to the freight cars. The crowd was big, and it was tough to get in. There were no steps to climb, and the cars were high up. Women stepped on one another and climbed on others' backs to get in. The noise was deafening; there were blows, screaming, and shoving— the fight for survival had reached a new high point.

And over it all, there was the barking of the dogs, the clubs of the Germans, and their shouts: "Hurry up, hurry up!"

Hands lifted me high. My mother's hands? I didn't know. Someone shoved me on and I fell to the cold floor of the car. Dolka managed to get into the car after me; she was pulling my mother along behind her, holding on to her hand. The car was full, but the blitz maidens ordered us to squeeze in tighter. More women were forced inside.

I had gotten back onto my feet. Dolka and my mother were tightly packed in beside me. I was jammed in among the women. I could hardly breathe, and my arms were pressed up against my body. Then, suddenly, someone clambered up onto my shoulders and pushed me down. I tried to get free, to stand up, but a heavy boot stepped on my head. I yelled and struggled to evade the boot, but I didn't succeed. The crush was so great, I couldn't move. I couldn't even raise my hand. The heavy pressure on my shoulders and head hurt, and my mother, on whom women were also standing, told me to be brave. "Stay standing," she ordered. "It won't last for long; it's not a long journey."

The big iron door was closed with a bang. Outside, we could hear screams and gunshots. The cars lurched; the train began to move.

The train's motion caused the women on top of us to lose their balance. They fell and lay on top of us or between us. The crush was tremendous. The heavy shoe on my head disappeared and the weight on my shoulders lessened. I tried to catch some air, but it was warm and stifling in the car, and of course it stank, too. I felt as if I were suffocating.

Out of sheer terror, the women couldn't keep from relieving themselves. After all, it was already afternoon, and we hadn't been given the opportunity to go to the bathroom since five that morning.

We didn't know how long the train ride lasted; perhaps

one hour, perhaps two, but it was an eternity for us. And when the train did stop, we remained locked up in the closed freight cars for many more hours. We stood in the heat and the stench, we could hardly breathe, and we were suffering from the lack of space and from hunger. But thirst was the worst thing. Because of the departure, we had received nothing to eat or drink that morning. Anyone losing consciousness remained propped up among the others; there was no room to fall down. Only urine and feces fell to the floor to increase our suffering.

The women who stood beside the grated window reported that we had arrived at a harbor. A ship lay at anchor. The high-ranking officers and the other German travelers were boarding it. Only after they were aboard were the doors of our cars opened; soldiers pushed us to make haste: "Out, out! Hurry up, hurry up!"

With benumbed limbs, we sprang from the cars and ran onward, pushing and shoving. We left many women unconscious or dead on the floors of the freight cars behind us.

The dogs were barking. From time to time clubs came down on heads or shoulders, but we were running to the shore without raising our heads or looking about us. Before us lay a big, white ship whose dark shadow fell upon the shore. Once again we had to line up on the dock, in the shadow of the ship. After being counted we got the order to board the ship. One after another we ran along a narrow board that led up to the stern deck. For an instant I could see the whole deck right up to the bow: only kapos, soldiers, and SS men, as far as I could see.

After running fast, and before we could draw a full breath of the damp sea air, we were again forced to make haste and climb down a ladder into the ship's hold, where cargo was normally stowed.

I don't know how many cargo decks our ship had; I believe the third was the lowest, at any rate. In the middle of the topmost cargo deck there was a large opening. Usually chests and crates of cargo would be lowered through it with a crane. Through this opening we were now sent down into the ship's belly. We climbed down a long ladder into the storage area assigned to the women—the lowest cargo deck. Many women slipped and fell. They remained lying on the deck where they fell.

It was dark down below. The deck was covered with straw, and the ceiling was so low you could only stand bent over. We climbed down among the first group. I wanted us to look for a place in a far corner, by the wall. But my mother wanted to remain closer to the opening. She was hoping it would be lighter there, and that more air would get in. Maybe we would also be able to hear what was happening above. When all the women had climbed down to the cargo room, it was so crowded we had no room to stretch out our legs. The ladder was pulled up and part of the opening was covered. The men prisoners were then loaded into the deck above us, pushed together like a herd of cattle. Once again the ladder was raised and the opening above closed halfway.

Darkness enveloped us. After standing crushed together for hours, we now lay on the damp straw as if we were stunned. Tightly packed one next to another, we tried to stretch our aching limbs. We were hungry; we hadn't had a bite, nor anything to drink, the whole day. I lay between my mother and Dolka. Next to us lay Rachel and Marila, Fienia, Dascha, Batja and Mascha Efron, and Helga, my friend from Kaiserwald, with her mother.

We were silent. The terrible day behind us had left its mark. Only now were we noticing that the weak and sick women who had been taken away from the camp that morning hadn't reached the ship.

Many of the women who had left the camp with us were now also missing: everyone who hadn't been able to cram into the freight cars; everyone who had remained, suffocated, back in those cars. The sudden discovery—that so many women who had been with us in Kaiserwald for the last year hadn't survived the evacuation—filled us with grief and pain. Once again we had received a sign of just how helpless we were. And—once again—an unknown future lay before us.

Suddenly the noise of engines was heard, and movement could be felt. The noise grew to a deafening racket; the floor of the ship trembled, and we trembled with it. The women woke up and began to talk with one another, but you could hardly hear anything over the all-encompassing din. Daylight fell through the opening in the deck; the ship got underway. Where were we going now? And who among us would be alive at our destination?

A couple of hours later a few overseers and kapos came to the opening and brought boxes with some bread and dried, salted meat with them. They threw the rations of bread and meat in all directions, and we had to catch them. A fight broke out over the bread. We were very hungry and the food—especially the dried meat, which we hadn't seen for more than a year—made our mouths water. We began to eat immediately, enjoying the taste of the tough salted meat. I sucked on the last piece of it for a long time.

The women were complaining that there was no toilet. The kapos promised to look for a remedy. The mood improved a little, despite the noise and the rolling motion of the ship. A few men and women went climbing up to the upper decks. They would be carrying out various tasks assigned to them during the trip.

It wasn't long before it was clear to us we had been viciously deceived. The dry, salted meat we had eaten made us very thirsty. Since we had received no water that entire day, we were suffering greatly. Women were groaning and sighing, but there was no water. The thirst was worse than the hunger. The women could not bear it any longer and began crying loudly. After their mouths ran dry from crying and screaming, they could only whimper. The noise of the engines, accompanied by the quiet whimpering, grated on our nerves.

But the solution our tormentors found for the toilet problem was even worse. With a block and tackle, they lowered down a few buckets, and we set them up in three different corners. The women stood in long lines in order to relieve themselves. The buckets filled up quickly. We then had to bring them to the opening and secure them to the dangling rope, with which they would finally be hauled up.

The ship rolled, and the full bucket swayed on the rope. Its contents slopped out and flooded over the floor. After the bucket had been dumped into the ocean, it came back by the same route, filthy and stinking. When it reached the deck, the next bucket was already waiting to be hauled up. Feces sprayed everywhere. Sometimes, when the bucket hadn't been securely fastened to the rope, or when the people above had had enough of their work and let go of the rope, all its contents overturned on us. A suffocating stench arose. Those of us who lay near the opening suffered especially. We tried to get away and scrunch ourselves back into a corner, but without success.

As we got farther from the harbor and reached the open sea, the rolling of the ship grew worse, and so more urine and feces got slopped. And with the greater rocking of the ship, the vomiting began.

The lack of air, the stench, and the thirst were unendurable. Slowly, now, seasickness was growing, and more and more women began to vomit. The buckets were full, and you couldn't get to them. Women lay on top of one another and vomited on themselves and on their neighbors.

Hysteria broke out among the women and they lost their wits. I lay curled up in a ball beside my mother. I was unable to relieve myself out in the open; under no circumstances could I do so in such a nauseating bucket. For two days now I had not had a bowel movement, and I was suffering from stomach pain. I was very thirsty, and now I too began throwing up. I was seasick and I couldn't stop vomiting.

My mother, the weaker of the two of us, was by some miracle one of the few who didn't have to throw up. With a few other women, she helped Frau Dr. Resnik care for the sick women. They couldn't actually help much, for there was no medicine, no water, and no means of bettering the circumstances. They could do nothing but comfort and encourage the ill. They wiped up the vomit and feces with rags. That was also the reason my mother was permitted to climb up the ladder. After a while she came back down and brought wet cloths to wipe the deck.

After she had finished this work, she came back to us. Dolka was crying; she was feeling awful. My mother wiped off her mouth with a wet cloth she had secretly brought back to us, so we could clean up a bit. She told us what she had seen abovedecks. It was a beautiful, bright day, and the air was clear. The ship was full of Germans who were strolling about, drinking and eating and in a good humor because they had succeeded in escaping from the Red Army at the last minute.

They were the families of superior officers who had managed to leave Riga before the entrance of the Russians. They had joined the ship that was transporting the last prisoners. Naturally, they had every reason to be glad. The ship was sailing under the flag of the Red Cross. My mother hadn't been able to learn where the voyage was bound, only that it would last about two days. She encouraged us and said that we surely had the roughest part of the trip behind us.

My mother had heard from the men that two foreign

submarines had approached us in the night. Presumably they were Russian, and the Germans were afraid they would attack us. But after the Russians had seen the flag of the Red Cross, they had come no closer. Instead, they had only sailed alongside us. We felt so dreadful, we almost wished that the submarines had attacked the ship and that we had gone down with the German officers. We longed for an end to our suffering. And our tormentors would have died with us.

During the night between the second and third days, the waves died down. Worn out and exhausted from two terrible days, most of the women slept. Despite the noise of the engines, it became somewhat quieter on our deck.

German doctors, accompanied by doctors from among the male prisoners, came down and examined the women on our deck on the morning of the third day aboard ship. We were suffering terribly from thirst. The vomiting and diarrhea caused by the cured meat had led to life-threatening dehydration, and many women were unconscious. The prisoner doctors examined the poor wretches and found a great number of dead among them. The corpses were now hauled up in the same way the buckets of feces had been raised. Bodies rolled and swayed above our heads.

Most of the dead were only half dressed; the women who lay near them had undressed them and taken their shoes and clothes for themselves—anything they might need in the future. But what would the future bring us? Despair without end?

Suddenly a woman began praying quietly. She was saying the *Sh'ma Yisrael*.* I didn't know the prayer; nor did the

---

* *Sh'ma Yisrael* (Hebrew): "Hear, O Israel," the declaration of the singularity of God. The *Sh'ma Yisrael* is read daily in morning and evening services, and is also the final profession in the hour of death.

women about me. Most of them weren't religious, but at this moment, the words were passing from mouth to mouth: "*Sh'ma Yisrael . . .*"

When the whispering reached us, my mother, Dolka, I, and all the women about us began to repeat the incomprehensible words. Like our common suffering, the prayer bound us together. It was the first time in my young life that I had heard that prayer. It encouraged us, it strengthened us, it comforted us, even if only for a short time.

I had been constantly vomiting during the whole voyage. Vomiting that much, without having had anything to eat or drink during the past three days, was hard to endure. At the beginning I had vomited vast amounts of liquid, then only bitter, yellow gall; and at the end nothing more came out. But the suffocating feeling of having to vomit had tortured me the whole time. For three days I hadn't slept, because of the constant vomiting, and I hadn't stirred from my spot. I had lain on the filthy straw and heard the noise about me without being able to react, or take part in what was going on around me. Then, finally, I fell asleep.

I didn't know how long I had slept, but at least half the night, right up to the morning. My mother woke me up and said the ship had stopped moving. After a voyage of four days the engines were silent. We were once again afraid and didn't understand what was up. Silence fell over us. We could feel the ship had stopped rocking. Only the murmur of the water and the slap of the waves on the ship's hull could be heard. We knew we had arrived at our destination. We lay in the filth and the stink and waited.

Then we suddenly heard voices and noise from the upper deck, the calls of porters who were beginning to unload the baggage of the SS men and their families.

I wanted to go back to sleep, but my mother was having none of that. She urged me to make haste and said we had to make ourselves ready to disembark. That meant we had to pull ourselves together physically, and above all, mentally. When we got off the ship, we would have to give the impression of being healthy, strong women.

When the hole above us was opened, daylight streamed into our dark hole. My eyes hurt, and I perceived the people above us as mere shadows. They turned away in aversion when they smelled the cloud of stench that climbed up from our deck.

Rachel came over to me and said, "Susinka, once again a chapter of our lives is behind us. Once again we're turning a new page. That last chapter we'll simply call *gówno* (shit)."

The ladder was lowered; this time nobody came down to us. With shouts and cries, we were ordered to climb up. "Out, out!"

The women stayed lying down; they simply had no strength and they lacked the will to move. They hadn't the strength to stand up; their legs wouldn't obey them; their bodies were immobile. The legs of most of the women had swelled greatly. But the first ones began to move slowly. My mother was among them. She pulled me to my feet forcefully; she yelled at me; she yelled at Dolka; she yelled at the women about us.

"Rachel, get out quickly and breathe the fresh air. Get up, Dolka, and help me keep Susie on her legs. Susie, get up quickly; lean on me; come on, get up." And so on. Her yelling and her uproar had the effect of bringing me around. Out of habit, I obeyed her automatically and without asking anything.

I tried to stand up and immediately fell back down. I had no strength. Dolka succeeded in getting to her feet, and my mother helped me to get up onto mine. The two of them dragged me to the ladder. My mother shoved Dolka up first, then me. She herself came behind me, propping me up with her body. The last few rungs, she was pushing me up and practically threw me onto the upper deck.

The women crept out of the belly of the ship, like animals, like insects, one after another. The sun was shining; it was a beautiful, agreeable day. It was as if nothing bad had been happening in the world for a long time; as if there were no prisoners who now were crawling out on all fours from the underworld and into the light. We closed our eyes, groping our way forward like blind people. The light, the warmth, and the fresh air were beating down on us and waking new strength in us.

The Germans had a lot of difficulty restraining their dogs, who wanted to attack the creeping, stinking crowd moving past them. The officers, the guards, and even the kapos shrank back from the odor we emitted; they were alarmed by the terrible sight.

Despite the shouting and the barking, the stream of people from the realm of the dead moved on only slowly over the narrow gangway that led to shore.

When we had landed, my mother led our whole group to one side. We sat down and filled our lungs with fresh air. A short distance from us there was a puddle of water. My mother took me there and washed my face and hands. Soon other women came and we made room. Dolka wanted to drink from the puddle, but my mother raised her hand and shoved Dolka forcefully away. The water was salty and dirty; we were already suffering from stomach pains and diarrhea without it.

The place didn't look like a harbor. About us lay fields and little houses. Children approached and stared at us.

When the sun was high in the sky, soup pots were brought to us. The starving women mobbed the pots to get some of the food. I stayed seated in my place. Nothing interested me, not even the food. But my mother came back with two plates of soup. Karola, our blockhouse kapo from Kaiserwald, had been standing by the pots from which the food was distributed. She had asked my mother where I was, and when my mother pointed to me, she had immediately given her another serving of soup for me. It was hard for me to swallow; I got almost nothing down, but my mother forced me to take one swallow after another.

After eating, we were summoned to roll call. We could hardly stand, and one woman after another collapsed. After loud shouting by the Germans and kapos, and after the endless counting, it became evident that many women had been left behind on the ship—unconscious or dead. Following roll call we others were moved slowly along the shore. In about an hour, during which we had more crawled than walked, we came to a canal. There, already waiting, stood what were called "barques"—used for the transportation of goods. Five or six of these barques were to be towed by a barge.

The barques were narrow and deep, and crawling with German guards. We climbed in. It was so cramped belowdecks that you couldn't stand. We immediately sat down next to one another on the floor. The barques filled up slowly. The guards were driving the women on with the warning that anyone who didn't get in at once would be thrown into the water. At last the barge arrived that was to pull our train of barques; it was fastened to the front of them. There were living quarters for the crew on the barge; our guards also slept there. They relieved each other every couple of hours.

Toward evening bread was distributed, and something to drink: a cup of stale, cold tea that we drank greedily. We were already so thirsty that we were unable to chew the bread. It stuck fast to our gums. In the early evening our train of barques got underway; behind us another followed, with the men from Kaiserwald.

The women fell asleep sitting up. But I didn't feel good because of the water's swell, and began to vomit once again. My mother led me out. The guards had pity on me. They allowed me to sit above, on the edge of the barque, so I could simply puke into the water. The fresh air did me so much good that the desire to vomit subsided.

Although it was a cold night, I stayed outside, and my mother sat belowdecks, next to the exit, and never let me out of her sight. Other women began climbing out; one after another they squatted down, hanging out over the edge, in order to relieve themselves directly into the water. The German guards walked about among them.

I could hardly sleep because of the icy wind that blew in my face, but I was feeling much better. I stayed outside during the whole journey, which lasted three days. Twice a day we got bread and a warm drink, and from time to time a little water.

It was the final days of autumn. On both sides of the canal stretched a vast, lonely countryside. I dreamed I was journeying to foreign lands, to foreign peoples, where there was freedom and peace. There were nice moments on the journey, and I enjoyed the sights it afforded me.

During the day the sun was still quite warm, but when the sun went down, it grew cold. In the daytime I washed myself in the canal water. I lay down on the deck boards and trailed my hands or my feet in the water. Lying on our stomachs, we were also able to wash our underwear and our feces- and vomit-stained clothing.

I would hold in my hands the piece of clothing that my mother had just washed and let it be dried by the wind and sun. Then the clean piece of clothing was put back on and the next piece washed. Very few women did this. Almost all of them just lay there, indifferent and unable to stir. But my mother gave Dolka and her friends a good talking-to, and our group succeeded in collecting ourselves, washing ourselves, and reassuming a human appearance.

Despite all our precautions, we had a lot of lice in our garments. All of us suffered terribly from them. No amount of washing, or drying in the wind, or careful examining of the clothing seams, helped. The lice remained and multiplied on us.

We began to prepare ourselves for the new camp. My mother was worried about her appearance. Because her hair had turned completely white, she looked much older than she was. She took care to always wear a scarf about her head that hid her white hair. To her face she applied the rouge she still had from working in the clothing depot, in order to look healthier and younger. At this time she also decided that in the future, I should call her by her first name, Raja, and not Mama anymore, since it could be dangerous for both of us. She ordered me to begin calling her that immediately, so I could get used to it. This was very hard for me. The word "Mama" still gave me a feeling of security: something we had brought with us from home, something that only I possessed. When I called her Raja, I became one of her friends, one of the adults . . . and I still wasn't even twelve years old.

And I had one other big problem on the barque—the toilets. We had already been underway for a week; during the whole time I had had no bowel movement. On the boat I suffered from dreadful stomach pains. But I simply couldn't squat down on the edge of the boat, beneath the eyes of the German guards.

Each day I waited for night to fall, for it to become dark. But all my attempts were useless. I suffered terribly. All my thoughts were bent only on defecation.

...RATIONSLAGER S t u t t h o f Fartart:..............Ger.

...und Vorname: *Barich, Susanna*

...en am: *8 / 26* zu: *Bialystok / Polen*

...ort: *Vilna, Freiheit 18*

...f *Schürin* Rel.: /

...ngehörigkeit: *Polen* Stand:

...es Vaters: *Josef R.* Der Mutter: *Fanni geb...*

...ort: *Stutthof*

...e des Ehemannes/Ehefrau: /

...ort: Kinder: /

...bildung *Volksschule*

...sse: *mittel* Gestalt: *schlank* Gesicht: *oval* Augen: /

...*normal* Mund: *normal* Ohren: *hoch* Zähne: /

...*braun* Sprache: *polnisch, deutsch*

...lende Krankheit oder Gebrechen: *keine*

...dere Kennzeichen: *keine*

...enempfänger:

...tet am: *Sept 1944* wo: *am Orte*

...l eingeliefert: *1.10.44* 2. Mal eingeliefert:

...sende Dienststelle: *Lipstadt*

...

...le Vorstrafen: *keine*

...dische Vorstrafen: *keine*

... ...ir darauf hingewiesen worden, daß ...eine Bestra...
... ..ler Urkundenfälschung erfolgt, wenn sich die obig...
... ...ch erweisen sollten.

... v. g. u. Der Lagerkommand...

....

Susanne Rauch

NOTIFICATION CERTIFICATE FOR THOSE
DESIGNATED FOR DEATH

STUTTHOF

THE STUTTHOF CAMP had been established in June of 1939, even before the beginning of the war. It was in a demilitarized zone containing the free city of Gdansk. There the local Nazis had been preparing secretly for the war. They already had jails and had built a camp for Polish prisoners—political captives and academics—and for Jews.

For the camp, they had chosen a village that lay about thirty-six kilometers (twenty-two miles) east of Gdansk, in an area surrounded by water: on one side by the Vistula River, on the other side by swamps. On one side stretched canals leading to the ocean; on the other, the Baltic Sea.

The Germans had sought out this locale because escape from here was practically impossible. In addition to that, the "Kaschuben"—ethnic German farmers—lived in the environs.

On September 2, 1939, one day after the outbreak of war, the first two hundred prisoners had already arrived at the camp. From that time on, the Stutthof camp existed.

The camp had been built on damp terrain—a swamp covered only by a thin layer of topsoil. The climate was cold and wet. The swampy water was deficient in chalk, but contained a high concentration of salt and iron. It was an environment that promoted illnesses and especially hindered wounds from healing. Lack of food assisted the spread of diseases; the blows we received often left wounds behind them. In this region, they quickly became stinking sores.

The prisoners at Stutthof made up an international

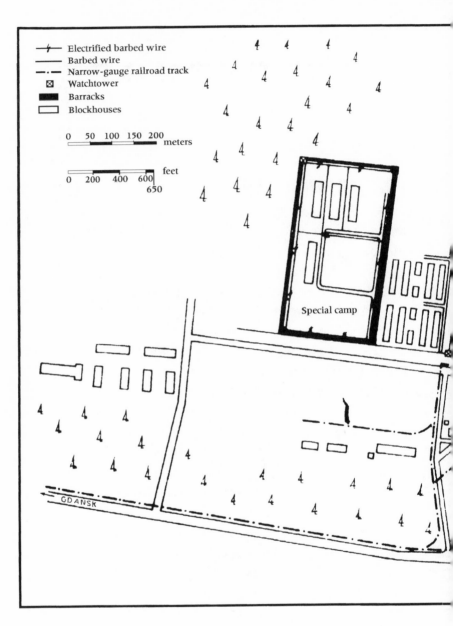

PLAN OF THE STUTTHOF CAMP—DEC. 31, 1944

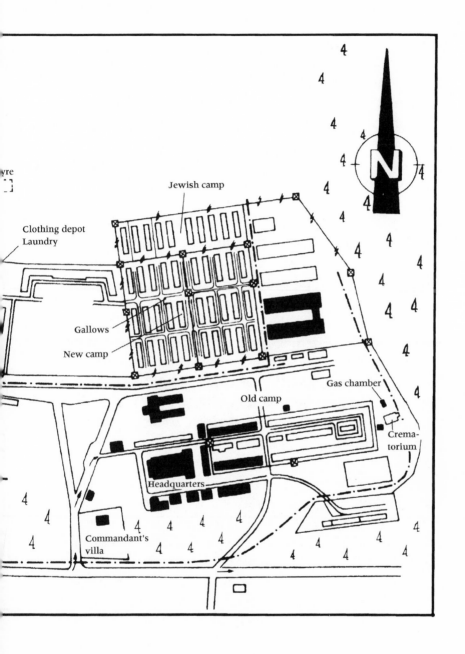

yre

Clothing depot
Laundry

Jewish camp

Gallows

New camp

Gas chamber

Old camp

Crema-
torium

Headquarters

Commandant's
villa

N

189

camp. Men in particular were held prisoner there. In the second half of 1944 the Stutthof camp became one of the camps involved in the "final solution," that is, the extermination of the Jews. Then the conditions in the camp, which were already terrible, grew even worse. The camp was simply unprepared to accommodate—even temporarily—all the people who were taken there by the huge transports.

At that time they also began transporting Jewish women there. The new camp was big. There were twelve Jewish blockhouses in its domain. These were extremely badly built, and in many cases not even finished. They had no floors; several even had no roofs. They were separated by barbed wire from the rest of the camp, and divided further into a men's and a women's camp. Originally, each had been designed to hold five hundred people; fifteen hundred to two thousand were now being housed in each blockhouse.

On October 1, 1944, we stepped out in orderly rows along the street between the canals. We passed the crossroads and turned into the camp. We passed the headquarters; we passed the well-tended area on our right. Then we entered the camp through the main gates, the "Gates of Death."

The intake began in front of the office, the orderly room. It was a cruel welcome. We were made to array ourselves for roll call. After they had counted us again and again, an officer appeared and gave a speech in German. His voice screamed and barked at the same time:

"From now on you are no longer people; you are numbers, only numbers. That is how we will call you and that is how you must answer—with your own number, and in German. From the moment you stepped through the gates, you lost every right; the only right remaining to you is to work for the German Reich. The only possibility you have of leaving here is to fly through the chimney."

With those words, he pointed his finger at a chimney

that could be seen at the end of the camp. Out of it rose black, stinking smoke. We now noticed, too, the peculiar, sweetish smell of burning flesh, a smell that immediately stuck to us and never left us until the end.

We stood on the roll call ground, the big square of the "old camp," which was hemmed in on two sides by blockhouses. To our left were the entrance gates and the rear of the headquarters; to our right a double barbed-wire fence with electric wires. All about the area stood watchtowers.

We had to stand there a long time as the officer and the kapos walked between the rows among us, considering us and seeking out the weak and the sick. Those were immediately led away in the direction of the chimney.

Row by row, we went into the command headquarters and were successively entered onto lists. Each one of us had to fill out questionnaires and sign them.

This time Raja filled out the forms: first, her own, then mine, and finally Dolka's, so that our numbers would be side by side and we could perhaps remain together. She entered my name as "Rauch" and named Bialystok as my place of birth. For my mother's name she gave the name of Dolka's mother. That way, I couldn't be identified as the daughter of my mother, that is, Raja's daughter.

She had also altered her personal data; she had made herself ten years younger. So I became an eighteen-year-old; Dolka was twenty, and Raja thirty. That way, we all fell into the same age group, the group entitled to live. We received the numbers 95382, 95383, and 95384. The usual procedures followed: showering and disinfection. Finally we were taken to the "new camp." There, in the square of the women's camp, we were placed in rows for roll call and counted again.

We heard a couple of transports of Jewish men from Estonia had arrived a few months ago. These men lived in the blockhouses bordering on the Jewish women's camp. Raja was quite excited. Perhaps she would learn something of Julek; perhaps he was even here, and she could see him.

Across the way, many men were gathering by a double barbed-wired fence through which ran electric cables. The men were a terrible sight; they looked like beggars. They wore completely ragged civilian clothing, on which a circle had been painted with oil paints. Their thin, gray faces were framed by cropped beards and stubble. Down the middle of their skulls, between their shorn hair, ran a two-centimeter shaved stripe, the "louse street." They staggered when they walked; they dragged their legs, and despair lay in their eyes. Frightened, each group considered the other: they, us; and we, them. All of a sudden a man recognized an acquaintance in our group and called her name. And then, again and again, other men also discovered women they knew.

The shadows who stood across from us, behind the barbed wire, were men from Vilnius, who had come to Stutthof from Estonia. When we got the "at ease" order, Raja went a few steps closer to the fence. Amid the sad cluster she in fact discovered her husband, Julek, and her brother, Wolodja. She stood as if stunned, and the tears spilled from her eyes. We were not permitted to go up to the fence; we were not permitted to speak with the male prisoners. That was all forbidden.

We were taken into the blockhouse. The blockhouse kapo was named Anna. She was a small, round Russian woman, with blue eyes and crinkly blond hair.

Three-tiered wooden bunks that more truly resembled cages stood in the blockhouse. On each of these bunks, eighty centimeters wide (less than three feet across), four or more women had to sleep. We got a place on the third tier. The bunks stood side by side, and many women were crammed into the awful narrowness.

Our part of the camp served as a transit camp; the

women there didn't work. For that reason, each day you had to stand for hours of roll call, out in the open, in rain and snow, in heat and cold.

A German doctor sometimes came and scrutinized the women. He went along the rows, considering the legs of each one and deciding from their appearance whether the women were worth keeping alive or not.

Day after day several dozen of the "sick" would be sorted out from among the rows of women and sent to the gas chambers, or they would be killed by injection. When the German doctor didn't find enough women with wounds on their legs at roll call, the whole group had to run in a circle; anyone who didn't make it through this fast running would be sent to her death.

We got only half food rations, because we weren't working. Hunger tormented us, and Raja looked for a solution. On our bunk we found a torn quilt filled with cotton. Raja thought the fabric of the quilt—a shiny, yellow satin— might be serviceable.

At the first opportunity she had to stand near Anna, she turned to the blockhouse kapo and, in Russian, proposed that she should make her a pair of pajamas out of satin. Anna enthusiastically embraced the idea, and "organized" a pair of scissors and a needle. Raja sat on the bunk; I helped her, and together, we separated the fabric from the quilt and carefully gathered up the threads. After this Raja washed the fabric and took it into Anna's room to dry. While it was still somewhat damp, she stroked it smooth, and finally laid it beneath our mattress.

The next day the fabric was smooth and looked as if it had been ironed. Raja cut it up and began sewing the pajamas by hand. For that she used the old threads. She took out the elastic band from her own underwear and inserted it into the pajama pants. After the pants had been sewn without a hitch, she started in on the top. She chose a straight pattern, with wide, side-cut kimono sleeves.

The work went well, and after a week Raja brought the present to Anna. In this manner she won herself a "friend." Raja asked Anna to transfer her to working as toilet attendant, and Anna gladly granted her wish. There weren't many who were volunteering to do this work; most of the women inhabitants suffered from diarrhea and dysentery, and the toilets were very dirty. The toilet attendant had to sit in the room with the toilet bowls all the time, paying attention to their cleanliness, cleaning the ten bowls, and making sure the women were orderly in their use of them. When Anna went to the bathroom, the attendant on duty had to bump all the women waiting on line and keep the toilet free for Anna's sole usage. At those times the blockhouse kapo would say, mockingly, "Make room, the queen is going to shit."

In this way Raja not only earned Anna's affection, but also got an extra ration of soup for herself, and one for me, as a result of her work. And after a bit she also even managed to secure an extra ration of bread. We ate the soup ourselves, but we tried to push the bread through the fence to Wolodja and Julek. Their situation was much worse than ours, since they had already been in this horrible camp for two months. Things were so bad in Stutthof that Kaiserwald now seemed like paradise to us.

The time dragged on. We did nothing, but it was forbidden to remain in the blockhouse during the day. We moved about the square between the blockhouses, stood for roll call, or sat leaning against the blockhouse walls.

From time to time we succeeded in getting closer to the fence and seeing the men from a distance. And sometimes, when a kapo wasn't close by, we were even able to throw them bread, or exchange a few words with them.

The men weren't working either, and we were terribly worried about them; from experience, we knew that only those who worked had a chance to stay alive.

My camp friend Helga became ill, and after I'd not seen her for a few days, I spotted her on the other side of the fence, at the window of the barracks that served as the Jewish infirmary. That building was called the "Blockhouse of the Dying" or the "Stink Room." I was terrified. I knew that in this camp, the sick weren't cared for; instead they were killed by injection. The corpses were burned in the crematorium—two chimneys smoked without interruption.

When I saw Helga, I forget all rules of caution. I ran on and neared the barbed-wire fence. I screamed and tried to speak with Helga. She stood behind the closed window and saw me, but she couldn't understand what I was saying. She waved at me. The conversation didn't last long.

One of the blitz maidens patrolling the area noticed me. She and "horrible Vera," the kapo of the neighboring blockhouse, came up to me, and the blitz maiden began to hit me with the club she held in her gloved hand. A rain of blows beat down upon my body and my head. I didn't cry out; I knew that my cries would only increase her cruelty. From experience we had learned to keep silent when getting a beating. When you kept quiet, those doing the hitting calmed down faster.

Out of the corner of my eye I saw Raja, who was standing together with her friends Rachel, Marila, Fienia, and Batja; but none of them approached me. They stood there and observed the scene, the same as the other women in the square. The blows drummed on, accompanied by the shouting of the German. I fell to the ground and she continued to beat me but then, suddenly, her hand caught on something and her watch came loose and fell down. At that moment the SS woman calmed down. She swore coarsely in

German, picked up the watch, and screamed at Vera to punish me.

The German left the square. I stayed lying on the ground. Vera called one of the women and ordered her to fetch a bucket of water and empty it over me. The cold splash of water brought me to my senses; I pulled myself together and tried to get up. Vera dragged me behind her to the center of the square. Three stools designated for the punishment of prisoners stood there. Vera ordered me to climb up on one of the stools. I did so. Vera left the square and went into her blockhouse. I remained standing on the stool in the middle of the square. At a distance I saw Raja, who was looking over at me.

I stood on the stool for hours. My body hurt, and I was so dizzy, the world turned about me. But all I could think of was: I have to keep standing; I have to stay upright if I want to stay alive. I read that in the eyes of my mother, who was staring at me unblinkingly. I stood on the stool until midday. Only after the food had been brought did Anna come out of our blockhouse and order me to get down from the stool and go into our blockhouse.

Inside, I stumbled next to the first bunk. I had no strength to climb onto the bed. Raja came and brought me two plates of soup, but I couldn't eat anything. My whole body hurt. Raja brought a wet towel and cleaned my wounds and my bumps. Then she laid me down on the first bunk near the entrance. I immediately fell asleep. I slept and slept. The next morning it was hard for me to wake up and go to roll call. Anna listed me as sick, and allowed me to stay in bed the whole day. Slowly I recovered.

One day a transport arrived with women and small children. We became witness to horrible scenes as they wrested the children from their mothers. Everything we had lived through long before, we now suddenly saw again. Shocked by these scenes, the whole camp seemed to groan and sigh. It was as though the world would collapse beneath the wordless lamentations, the bitter tears, and the heart-rending cries.

At the end of October a group of officers from the German army appeared in the camp. They set themselves up in the middle of the square. We were ordered to leave the block-houses and go to the square. All at once one of the officers ordered all the seamstresses to step forward. Raja grabbed me by the hand and wanted to step forward. But other women had been quicker, and had stepped forward earlier. The officer chose fifteen women. We were not among them. Then the officer announced he needed upholsterers, and again Raja stepped forward. She had no luck this time, either. Now the officer wanted furriers. The women hesitated, and Raja seized the opportunity. She ran to the officer, pulling me along behind her. She was skilled in working with furs, she said, and I was her chief assistant. She couldn't work without me. But the officer needed still more furriers. Raja encouraged all her friends to sign up for this work. Only Dolka refused to go along. She didn't want to work for the Germans anymore. Her condition had become noticeably worse; for some time we had felt that she was changing into a Mussulman before our eyes.

The skilled workers—about forty—chosen by the officer for work in a shop lined up in three rows and left the Jewish women's camp under guard.

We went to work. Our workshops were in heated barracks, and our work involved repairing fur coats for the German army.

We set out each morning. We got our midday meal in the workshop: a thicker soup than you got in camp, and an extra ration of bread. Raja and I saved some of the bread and passed it on to the men from time to time. At night we went back to the camp to sleep.

On the road to work (and at danger to our lives), we sometimes succeeded in "organizing" some frozen sugar beets that had been left lying on the fields. We put these beets on top of the oven of the workshop until they were baked. They tasted delicious.

A very hard winter began, but we were protected in the warm workshop. Raja was the supervisor of our work crew. We were repairing fur jackets sent back from the front with bullet holes. They were often flecked with blood. When a big shipment of torn jackets arrived, we were very happy.

One day Raja informed the German in charge that the electric wiring in our blockhouse was defective. She proposed he fetch from the men's camp an electrician who was knowledgeable about such repairs. She recommended Wolodja to him. The officer agreed. In his capacity as electrician, Wolodja was able to move freely among the workshops, and so he came to us, too. Our reunion was very moving. We told him everything we had gone through, and also that his wife, Chassia, and his daughter, Fejgele, had gone to the left.

We saw him almost every day, for Raja was always discovering new problems with the power supply. She would make something in the sewing machines break and then have Wolodja come and repair them. He ate with us, and we gave him bread to take with him to Julek. When the officer in charge entered the workshop, he would find Wolodja standing on the table, repairing a cable up on the ceiling.

Wolodja told us of the camps in Estonia. His brother-in-law had been killed there. He forwarded greetings to Marila Krinski from her husband. He had been in Stutthof a month ago, and had then been taken to a neighboring camp.

He told Fienia of her husband, who had been murdered, and of her son, who was somewhere in the neighborhood of Stutthof. Wolodja was very worried about how Julek had been behaving recently. He had lost his will to live; he suffered terribly from hunger, and his legs were swollen. Julek was a broken man, and Wolodja was afraid he would become a Mussulman. In the evenings, when we saw Julek standing at the fence that separated us, wrapped up in a blanket, Raja scolded him. But we had the impression that it was already too late, and that nothing would help anymore. Julek hardly listened to us; his interest was fixed only on the bread that we passed on to him.

On Christmas Eve of 1944, on the main roll call ground of the old camp, the Germans put up a beautiful Christmas tree. It was big and decorated with colored candles. All the prisoners of the old and the new camps were called to roll call late in the evening. This roll call lasted for hours. Suddenly a young Pole was brought into the middle of the square. Only then did we realize that a gallows had been erected next to the festively decorated tree.

After the officers had conversed for a long time and had abused the youth over and over, he was hanged in front of all eyes. On the eve of that high Christian holiday the prisoners were made to view the hanging—as if the Germans wanted to let us know that the cruelty would not stop, despite the holiday. The young man had been condemned to death for the theft of bread.

At the beginning of 1945, shortly after New Year's Day, two young Russians, two brothers, were hanged on the same gallows. The younger of the two had just turned fifteen. He cried and screamed and begged for mercy, but his older brother was quiet and self-possessed. Only in the last seconds of his life did he call out in Russian for vengeance. The Germans made an effort to drown out his voice by shouting, but we who stood on the roll call ground heard the words of the young Russian, even though we stood at some distance and couldn't see the pair. What he had said gave us new courage. He shouted, "The Red Army is already at the gates of Gdansk! They will come, free us, and avenge the blood that has been spilled!"

The cold increased, and it began to snow. The Germans decided it was too difficult to take the work squads through the heavy snow to the workshops each day. So beds were set up and we stayed overnight in the workshops. It's true we had to work late into the night, but despite that, we were happy with this arrangement, for the stoves were also kept burning at night there.

The winter of 1944–45 was especially severe. It snowed a lot, and the cold reached minus thirty degrees centigrade (twenty-two degrees below zero Fahrenheit).

On the twentieth of January we were suddenly taken back to the main camp. We returned to the same barracks. It was evident to us that many of the women who had been there a few weeks ago were no longer there. But we found Dolka again. She had gone downhill and was very weak. She looked like a Mussulman; her clothes were filthy and torn, and she had swollen legs. We tried to encourage her, and my mother often gave her some of her own bread ration, an almost unimaginable gift in that time of hunger.

Typhus spread through the camp. Each day there were dozens of dead. Morning after morning the women carried the night's dead out of the blockhouses and laid them down next to the wall. From there they were taken away on wagons beyond the fence. Since the crematoriums were no longer sufficient, they began burning the dead on a pyre. The pyre burned not far from the fence of the Jewish women's camp, and we could see it.

First, wood was piled up, and then corpses on top, then wood again, and so on. Once the pile had reached a height of about five meters (sixteen feet), the Germans poured fuel over it and set it on fire.

The burning pyre looked as if devils were dancing on it. As the wood burned, the corpses contracted, and suddenly the dead were moving: raising their hands and feet, bending over and sitting up; and sometimes a stream of water—urine—shot into the fire. We stood there staring at the pyre; some prayed quietly for the souls of the dead.

And then, all of a sudden, the liquidation of the Stutthof camp began. At the evening roll call of January 25, 1945, the evacuation of the camp was announced, and convoys were arranged for transportation. Once again Dolka refused to go with us. This time she said it was because of her father, whom she sometimes saw through the fence. She believed that Julek would surely not go, and for that reason she also didn't want to leave the camp.

I cried and begged Dolka to come with us. Perhaps Julek *would* go too, and we could see him on the way.

During the last roll call Raja held Dolka's hand, and when—at midnight—we were sent to the showers, she tried to take my stepsister with her. But Dolka refused.

She said loudly, "I can't go on." And to the officer who was standing nearby, she said, "I am sick; I want to stay here."

With the tip of his crop, the officer shoved her out of line to the other side, and pushed Raja on into the group that would go on the evacuation march.

I screamed, "Dolka!" I saw her for one more instant and our gazes met; then she disappeared into the gray mass of women who stayed behind on the roll call ground.

THE
DEATH MARCH

SNOW, FROST, ICE, BITING COLD—none of these words even comes close to expressing what I experienced when I stood outside, naked, on the night of January 25–26, 1945.

An hour earlier we had been hustled from the showers with cries of, "Out, out!" Using their clubs, they had thrashed us out of the warm, damp room in which we had just showered. As always the water had been either too cold or too hot, and it had run much too short a time, anyway. As it was stopping, the door was suddenly thrown open; snow and ice swirled in and brought freezing cold with them.

None of us wanted to go out into the cold and dark. But the blitz maidens and kapos had anticipated that and used the advantage of surprise. With sudden cries, with dogs, and with blows, they had hustled us onto the square.

It was night; it was dark, and the sky hung black and menacing above us. In the cold the stars glittered especially brightly.

Wet, naked, and barefoot as we were, we soon pushed tightly together, and the frost enveloped us. As always Raja tried to find a solution; she found a gap and shoved me in among the other women. I was no longer smaller and thinner than everyone else, for all the women were small and thin, with sunken breasts; nothing more than skin and bone. It was a miracle, but I had grown up recently, and all the other women, including Raja, had shrunk down. You

202

could no longer tell I was a child just by looking at my body.

My skin was transparent, my legs were gaunt, crooked, and long, and my arms looked as if a heavy weight had pulled them down and elongated them. My body, too, was only skin and bones; a small body compared to its limbs, with the shoulder bones sticking out starkly, and ribs that you could count. On my thin neck, which looked as if it could break at any moment, sat a much-too-large head, with a small face and overlarge eyes. My head seemed so large because I always had my turban on; I didn't even take it off in the showers. It was wrapped up high and made my small head look deformed—as if it didn't belong to me.

This time, too, in the whole rush and tumble, no one had paid any attention to the curious construction on my head, and so I had succeeded in holding on to it.

I found myself in the midst of a cluster of women who were trying to warm one another by rubbing their naked bodies against each other. The cold had enveloped us, but the worst cold came from below.

We were standing on snow and ice; our feet were naked and we couldn't stand still; the cold burned our soles. And so we hopped from one foot to another; in the crush, we often stepped on the feet of others.

Raja wouldn't allow me to stop and made me hop uninterruptedly and not leave either sole too long on the ice. I didn't yet understand why I had to keep moving, but I immediately felt a foot begin to freeze when I left it on the ice a second too long. The terrible cold compelled us to keep moving, and when a gust of air forced its way in among our bodies, the cold cut us to the bone.

Sometimes I was pushed aside by the hands of the women who stood outside the circle and who were trying to get in. We shoved and were shoved; without rest, we shoved and were shoved. The water drops that had remained on our skins when we came out of the showers into the icy cold had long ago dried from the natural warmth of our bodies. Raja stayed beside me the whole time and fought for a place in the tangle of bodies, for both of us. She rubbed my back with her ice-cold hands and urged me to keep moving.

But I didn't want to go on. Suddenly I cracked. The cold was unimaginable. It seemed to me that the cold was not only spreading on my skin; that it wasn't only my legs that had become so feelingless, it didn't matter to me whether someone stepped on them or not; that not only my hands were so frozen that I could no longer move them—I was also cold inside, in my stomach. The cold pushed through my body toward the inside. The shivering and the goose-flesh were only outward signs.

The skin on my forehead contracted and hurt; I couldn't lower my eyebrows and smooth my forehead; the skin of my head was too small for my skull, and although my head was still at least protected from the cold air by the turban, my head and my brain seemed as if they were frozen.

The worst was the pain in my chest, a pain that hindered me from breathing, as though my chest had been tightly laced up. This pain brought me to tears. The tears froze on my cheeks, and my skin hurt even more. I didn't want to go on!

I whispered to Raja that I wanted to sit, to let myself sink down onto the ice, among the legs of the women. And Raja, despite her despair, despite the cold of her own body, had to fight against me. She shook me with her strong hands; she hit me in the face with all her might and screamed, "Shut up! Stop crying! Jump; move; wave your hands; don't breathe with your mouth open!" And so on, and so on.

I was accustomed to obeying in such situations, and so I continued to move. When we got to the edge of the tangle,

Raja flung her arms about her body and began to hit herself quickly with both her arms and her stiff hands.

"This is what the coachmen in Siberia do," she said.

I followed her example. So did the women about us.

We could breathe only with difficulty, and although Raja had ordered me to breathe through my nose, I wasn't able to and had to breathe through my mouth. In the meantime other wet, naked women had just been driven out of the showers to us.

Once again inside the tangle, I was trying to stand next to women who were taller than I, so that at least from above I would be somewhat shielded from the cold air.

Because of the cold, we had to urinate over and over, and even I couldn't hold back. While they were standing packed tightly together, the women let their water run down over their own legs and those of the others. Nobody was bothered by it; on the contrary—the urine was warm, and for a brief moment, a blessed moment, it warmed our feet.

The hours went by; I couldn't count them. Again and again Raja said this was probably our final tribulation, for we had heard that the front was no longer far away from us. She comforted me: "It's good the wind off the ocean isn't so strong today; it's good it's not snowing tonight." And so on.

No, it wasn't snowing that night; that night there was no wind. The air was frozen and so stiff it seemed you could cut it with a knife. It was minus twenty-five degrees centigrade (thirteen degrees below zero Fahrenheit).

One woman crumpled to the ground and could no longer rise. Another broke down. Hands stretched out to haul them back up, but it was too late; they could no longer be helped. Finished.

In the early-morning hours, after the unendingly long

night, our clothes arrived from being disinfected. Petrified, our bodies glazed by a thin layer of ice, we went to the cart where our clothes were being distributed. One after another, each got her bundle. A couple of women, a couple of "lucky ones," also took the bundles of the women who would no longer need them.

Raja rubbed my body with snow, and we dressed quickly. She also rubbed my frozen feet. I could no longer feel them, and I couldn't put on my shoes. But with the help of another woman we found a pair of big, beat-up boots—men's boots, soldier's boots—that no one laid claim to. I stuck my stiff feet into those boots; I simply shoved them in. Given the circumstances, it was impossible for me to put shoes on any other way. And although our thin clothes were insufficient protection against the cold, we still felt more secure now.

A hot drink was distributed—thin tea, but at least it was hot. We drank, and warmed our hands and fingers on the tin bowls. Our noses and foreheads were also somewhat warmed by the hot steam.

Just then, after I had already gotten dressed, I was seized by a fit of shivering, an involuntary attack of trembling so severe I could hardly stay on my feet. Raja spoke to me, but I didn't answer; my voice had frozen and no sound came out.

The morning grew gray. The stars grew pale, and we were still standing on the square—over a thousand women, after the worst night of our lives. Shadows began to stir about us. The camp was waking up. It was probably five o'clock in the morning.

Next to the barracks with the showers was a blockhouse of German Catholic nuns. They wore civilian clothing; you knew they were nuns only because of the special way they wound their scarves about their heads, so that their foreheads were fully covered.

These women had seen us when we had arrived the previous evening, and now they were watching us through the window of the blockhouse. Their eyes were filled with pity; they were crossing themselves furtively. Throughout the night a couple of the nuns had probably been standing watch at the window, to witness our suffering and to pray quietly.

One after another they now came out and tried approaching us, but the guards chased them back.

Suddenly a motorcycle appeared, and behind it a black automobile with the commanders of the camp and the officers. We got the order to line up in rows of four and to begin moving in the direction of the main gates.

I was still trembling and didn't want to move. Raja was trying to shove me forward and get me walking. At that moment a small, shriveled-up nun pushed her way to our side and wound me in a very big woolen scarf. Raja thanked her quickly, but the little woman had already disappeared. Raja arranged the scarf over my head and my shoulders and hips, and then we got underway and went out through the gates of the Stutthof camp.

Thus began the death march.

All in all, over eleven thousand people set out marching in columns. A further eleven thousand from Stutthof and the surrounding camps were assigned transportation by small ships. It was the last ride for most of them: Anyone who didn't die of hunger and thirst went down with the ships, which were bombed not only by the Allies but also by the Germans.

We left Stutthof on the twenty-sixth of January, but the liquidation of the camp had already begun about four A.M. on the morning of January 25, with a roll call for the entire camp. The roll call had lasted a very long time; in the course of it, those slated for evacuation had been singled out.

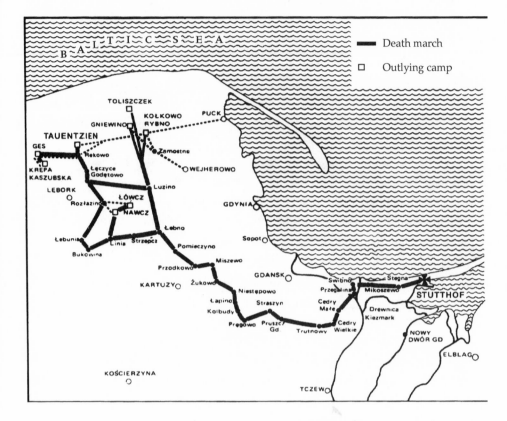

THE ROUTE OF THE DEATH MARCH

After disinfection the people were arranged in rows, and the columns set out on the march:

Polish men, Lithuanians, Letts, French, Russians, and Germans from Blockhouses I and II, numbering over sixteen hundred people, went as the first column. These were considered privileged, and they were joined by prisoners who had worked in the Jewish hospital.

The second column was comprised of men from Blockhouses III and IV; most of them were Polish and Russian prisoners of war; all together thirteen hundred fifty men.

The third column was men from Blockhouses V and VII: Poles, Russians, Danes, Czechs, Germans, and Norwegians, numbering fourteen hundred prisoners.

The fourth column was composed of Poles and Russians from Blockhouses VIII and X, totalling twelve hundred fifty men—all weak prisoners and sick people.

In the fifth column were Polish, Russian, Italian, and German Jews from Blockhouses IX and XIII, all together eleven hundred men. Wolodja and Julek were in this column.

The sixth column, from Blockhouses XII and XV, contained mostly Polish prisoners and a few Russians.

The seventh column (and the last to get underway on the night of January 25) was made up of women from the first blockhouse of the old non-Jewish camp. There were nine hundred women prisoners from all the diverse nations in the camp.

The next day, January 26, at three A.M., eight hundred twenty men got underway: Norwegians, Poles, Russians, and Frenchmen.

On the same day, at about six in the morning, yet another column set out. This was the ninth, and it had thirteen hundred women from the new camp, most of them Jewish.

Raja and I were in that column.

I learned this tally only much later. On that day, January 26, 1945, I didn't know how many people had left the camp. It seemed to me the whole camp was marching; the whole world was marching; all of humanity was marching. We passed through the last gate of the Stutthof camp; I remembered that as a welcome when we had arrived there, I had heard these words: "The only possibility you have of leaving here is to fly through the chimney."

Stiff from the cold, ill, and depressed, we went through the gates, but still—we were alive. Raja, who always managed to find encouraging words even in the toughest times, turned to Rachel, her best and closest friend in camp, and said, "You see, Rachel, up to now, we have won. We've left the Stutthof camp alive and on our own two feet."

We all turned around one more time and threw a last glance at the camp.

A new path into the unknown began. Could it get even worse? We doubted it. In the same way she always did, Rachel said, "Susie, we're ending a chapter. We're starting a new page."

Beyond the gates each of us got a blanket, a half kilo (just over a pound) of bread, and a half packet of margarine. Most of the prisoners were so starved that they immediately ate up their ration. Raja took over my ration and divided it up into several slices. How she had gotten a knife, I don't remember. Perhaps she had only borrowed it from another woman. At any rate, she cut the bread into slices and we each ate two.

The march had been planned by the Germans for an earlier date—for the beginning of January. But because of the approaching front and the big Soviet offensive that had begun in the area on January 12, the appointed day had been postponed. On the day of our departure the Soviets were thirty kilometers (about nineteen miles) away from us.

The commander of the march was SS Captain Theodor

Mayer. He commanded forty soldiers with revolvers, and SS men armed with machine guns.

Fifteen soldiers accompanied the two final columns on January 26, the second day of the march.

Additionally, there was a protective force comprised of twenty-five German soldiers with large German shepherd dogs that constantly ran back and forth. According to the plan, each column would put twenty-five to thirty kilometers (about fifteen to nineteen miles) behind them each day; their distance from one another would measure about two kilometers (about 1¼ miles).

The route passed through villages and small "Kaschuben" towns. The prisoners were to sleep in empty barns or stables, and warm food was also to be ready and waiting for them.

Those of us selected for the march were among the prisoners who, in the judgment of the camp's German officers, could endure the rigors of the march. But most of us were already infected with typhus. The camp leadership had repeatedly called upon the sick and the weak to remain in camp, but only a few had chosen to remain.

The going was tough for us. We walked more slowly than expected. The roads were covered in snow; in many places the snow was so deep, we sank into it. Many times the snow had to be removed before we could go on.

The trek was hard and exhausting. Even those who were healthy when we set out became weak and dragged their feet along behind them. Along with that, the cold was unbearable—minus twenty to twenty-five degrees centigrade (four to thirteen degrees below zero Fahrenheit). The cold wind off the ocean blew frozen snow into our faces. We tried to warm our hands beneath our clothing. The roads were clogged by fleeing German civilians.

Each commander of a prisoners' column was trying to find a route along side streets, in order to bypass the civilian populations. And so it happened that we fell behind and didn't reach the village assigned for our overnight rest. The guards broke into farmers' barns and stables so that we would have quarters for the night.

There was also no food for us. The supplies didn't arrive. We got absolutely nothing to eat the first days of the march. With cold hands, we gathered snow and drank the melt-water. As a substitute for food, we sucked on ice.

On the third and fourth days of the march, the weather became even worse; it began to snow heavily. We moved forward, covered in snow like mummies. I wrapped myself in the blanket and in the scarf I had gotten from the nun; I didn't leave even my nose out in the open. I didn't have to see the path; it was enough to follow whoever was walking in front of me. It was important to step directly in her foot-steps, so that I wouldn't sink into the fresh, soft snow.

The days were gray and gloomy, and it grew dark early. We had to continue our march in the dark.

"Hurry up, hurry up!"—"Keep together!"—"Close it up tightly!" We constantly heard these orders.

In the snowy, desolate fields, all sounds carried loudly. When we heard a gunshot, we knew once more that some-one hadn't made it; that someone had stumbled; that some-one had fallen down, or had simply gone too slowly and had fallen behind the column. The last person in each column was buffeted by the cold wind on his back; it took his breath away. His steps became slower and slower, and he lost con-tact with those ahead. When anyone fell too far behind, he lost his chance to catch up to the others; when the gap be-came large, he was simply shot by the soldiers who brought up the rear. The column following met up with fresh corpses.

When we heard the order to halt, we threw ourselves down by the side of the road and tried to stretch our painful limbs.

After a long day's march we reached a village. We had lost all sense of time or distance; we didn't know what stretch of road lay behind us or how many hours we had been going.

We halted before a tumbled-down barn. It wasn't large, but it was clear that we all had to get into it.

Everyone began to push and shove, to get under cover as quickly as possible and find a place to lie down. The soldiers hit the last ones with their rifle butts and shouted, "Hurry up, hurry up!" Those who were hit pushed the ones who stood in front of them farther in. I was afraid of the crush, and therefore we found ourselves at the end of the group fighting to get in. Raja shoved and tugged me. We knew that anyone who didn't get in would freeze out in the snow that night.

In despair, we were fighting for our lives. And when we finally got into the barn, we fought in the dark for a place to rest on the damp straw. The wind pressed in through the cracks and brought fine, cold snow with it.

When we came out the next day, toward morning, we found eight bodies in front of the barn. These were the women who had found no place in the barn; the ones who had lost the fight. (The Germans kept exact lists, and so we later learned that by the seventh day of the march, there were still about seven hundred thirty women alive out of the thirteen hundred who had set out.)

When we got underway again, many women had become so weak in the interval that they fell down by the side of the road. On both sides of the road, we saw the dead bodies of prisoners from the columns that were marching ahead of us. You could see that some of the dead had broken down and died from hunger and exhaustion; others had been shot, and the blood that flowed from their wounds stained the snow red.

Sometimes we were so close to the column ahead of us, we could see their shadowy figures staggering. We were also able to hear when the guards shot prisoners who had fallen behind. Often we even saw it happen.

The news of the death march spread quickly, and although the inhabitants of the region through which we passed were predominantly Nazis, still they didn't remain unmoved by the dreadful spectacle we presented.

On the morning of the eighth day of our march, the snow had suddenly been removed. Along the road were walls of snow in which, at certain intervals, big, thick slices of bread lay. The hungry women ran to the side of the road and threw themselves onto the snow in order to get the bread, but not many succeeded. When the guards noticed the disorder taking place in the column, they applied their machine guns, and a rain of bullets fell on those who had broken ranks. Not a few women fell dead to the ground, a piece of bread in their hands.

Raja had hurt her right leg when she had rushed off to grab a piece of bread. She had stumbled and fallen to the ground and cut her right shank on a sharp piece of ice. The leg swelled up and turned blue, and it became hard for Raja to walk. But the accident had saved her life. If she had reached the bread, she would no longer have been among us.

The call "Stutthof is marching" was spreading like wildfire among the natives. The train of shadows was attracting the attention of the people. They were gathering at the edge of the road, waiting in the cold and snow for hours. They had come from the farthest villages; they now stood there in silence, despite the attempts of our armed guards to drive them away.

In those days most of the civilians no longer had any fear of the SS. They stood there, angry, silent, and reproachful; a gray mass.

That same evening the natives brought big buckets of hot, thick soup to the church in which we had stopped for the night. It was a bean soup, with meat and bacon. We ate without spoons, from tin plates or cans. We drank the hot soup greedily; it burned our lips.

Our lips were cracked and torn from the cold and snow we had eaten, and during the night our wounds burned from the straw and filth in which we lay. Most of the women had open sores on their lips, and the festering wounds hurt.

My feet were also suffering terribly from the cold. I had blisters and sores from the uncomfortable, much-too-big men's boots, and from my torn stockings.

After an eleven-day march, after about one hundred twenty kilometers (seventy-five miles), what remained of our column—the ninth—reached Tauentzien* Camp. Tauentzien, a small town to the north of Lauenburg,** lay on a hill. Almost the entire area belonged to a wealthy German landowner, who was also mayor of the town. The forest behind his house belonged to him as well.

There in the forest the SS had built a work camp that was supposed to be used only in the summer, at harvesttime. Several small wooden barracks stood in the camp, which was fenced in with barbed wire.

We were taken there. Besides us women who were still alive after eleven days of the death march, there were also members of the fascist regime of Lithuania, who had been arrested toward the end of the war. They had turned against the Germans so as not to be pulled down into the coming ruin. In addition to these there were Norwegians, Letts, Finns, French, and Poles. Their columns had arrived before us and had occupied the best barracks at the site.

Because of the composition of the prisoners, "classes"

---

* Tauentzien: In Polish, Tawécin.
** Lauenburg: A town in Pomerania, now called Lębork.

sprang up here at the end of the world. Besides the Norwegians and Finns, the most privileged were the former members of the Latvian and Lithuanian regimes. These prisoners got water to wash in, and large rations of bread, bean soup, and cabbage.

The second group, the French, also got good soup, and were given the opportunity to work in the cattle stalls of the surrounding farmsteads. The Poles were isolated in the camp and got only one ration of bread and soup per day. We Jewish women had the worst of it.

The camp was actually a large rectangle, hidden among the trees of the forest. On one side stood the three good barracks. There were bunk beds in them with mattresses, blankets, and pillows. The fourth barracks of this row, which stood diagonally to the others, served as kitchen and storeroom.

When our six hundred women arrived, they stuck us into the two small barracks that stood by the road on the other side of the square. The winds were especially strong there. Our barracks was bare; there were neither bunks nor anything to cover ourselves with. Only fresh straw had been thrown into it.

All amenities were lacking in that part of the camp. Our barracks, the one on the road, had been erected in haste from old planks, with broad cracks between the individual boards. There was no floor; the straw covered the damp earth.

We had neither a well nor any other water supply. Drinking water was scarce, and we didn't even dare think of washing ourselves. There was also no sewer system in the camp, and the one latrine that was at our disposal was in the forest, behind the men's barracks. We could go there only as a group, under the supervision of the blitz maidens who guarded us.

There was such a lack of space that when the women

slept, we had to squeeze together like sardines. We all lay in a row, the length of the barracks' wall, and when one woman wanted to turn onto her other side, the whole row had to turn with her.

In the cramped space, and without any possibility of washing ourselves, the lice multiplied so rapidly they could no longer be controlled. The lice strolled over our faces and arms even in broad daylight, but they were especially active at night, when we were sleeping.

Day by day the food rations got smaller; there were no regular supplies to the camp, and the camp leaders soon were only looking after themselves. The prisoners had to satisfy themselves with the kitchen garbage.

Every couple of days we got a piece of black bread and a portion of soup. The soup was cooked from potato peelings or cabbage leaves, without salt. The peelings hadn't been properly washed; sand and dirt crunched between our teeth. The starving women sat in the barracks all day, dazed.

Because the hunger was becoming ever greater, the camp authorities brought in sick animals and dead horses and cows; soup was cooked from their flesh. Out of sheer hunger, the prisoners fell on the remains of the food that had been thrown out of the kitchen and fought over it. They even quarreled over the intestines of the dead animals.

Almost all the prisoners suffered from intestinal diseases and diarrhea with heavy bleeding; they began relieving themselves in every corner of the camp. Spotted typhus led to intestinal typhus and that led to a highly dangerous pathology. But there was neither a doctor nor any medicine in the whole camp.

The death toll climbed from day to day; first there were a few deaths, then, dozens. The dead were hauled out of the barracks each morning, taken to the forest, and thrown into a deep ditch. Quicklime was strewn over the corpses. There was no work in the camp, except cleaning the toilet of the camp authorities or disposing of the dead. It was wintertime, and farmers needed no workforce now; besides that, they were wary of contact with the camp inmates. The prisoners milled about the whole day; they had nothing to do and waited from one roll call to the next.

As always, Raja went looking for work, and found it, too. Women were needed to peel potatoes and wash the peelings in the prisoners' kitchen. When she heard that, Raja went running to the kitchen and was accepted for work.

She sat on the kitchen floor the whole day, working from the morning roll call until late in the evening. It was warmer in the kitchen; there was enough hot water to drink, and from time to time she could furtively stick a piece of washed potato peel or cabbage leaf into her mouth and chew it. Sometimes it might be the peel of a sugar beet or a red beet.

In the evening Raja would secretly bring me a few peels, but, most importantly, she now could give me some of her bread ration and soup, for she had already eaten a portion in the kitchen.

Unfortunately, the food didn't help me much. I was suffering from the bloody diarrhea called dysentery. The state of my health was constantly growing worse, and I could retain neither food nor water. Day after day I was growing more dehydrated. It finally came to the point where I didn't want to go to roll call anymore. Once again I was in danger of becoming a Mussulman.

Raja was completely perplexed, but she didn't give up. One evening she came back to the barracks with two completely charred potatoes. Along with them, she had also charred a piece of wood. Slowly, very slowly, she fed me the charcoal and gave me hot water to drink. A miracle occurred, and the diarrhea stopped after a few days.

I was nonetheless still very, very weak, and Raja was

afraid to let me eat the dirty soup. Now the final ring, which she still had hidden in a piece of soap, came into play. At the gates of the camp there sometimes stood a young SS guard who behaved more decently than the others. A couple of times he had smiled at Raja as she was going from the barracks in which I was lying to the kitchen where she was working. Once he had even said a few words in Russian to her. Raja decided to turn to him. When no one could be seen in the area, she grabbed the opportunity to start a small conversation with him.

His name was Georg. It turned out he was a Latvian of German ancestry, a so-called ethnic German. He had been forced to join the army, since they had threatened his family. He was only seventeen when he was sent here. He found guard duty in the camp very difficult, because he was dejected by the terrible conditions of the prisoners. But it was impossible for him to help the camp inmates, other than to behave in a friendly manner. He was glad he hadn't been sent to the front.

My mother offered Georg the ring for bread, but he had no bread that he could give her. He promised to scout around and look for a farmer who was willing to give food for the ring.

When the women of our group learned of this, they were terrified and scolded Raja for not being careful enough. Perhaps Georg would betray her to the camp authorities. But after two days Georg brought Raja a whole loaf of bread and a packet of margarine. That evening we ate the food in secret. One part of the bread Raja had given to Rachel, Fienia, Marila, and Dascha, but most of it was for me. After a few days Georg again brought a whole loaf of bread.

It's true my diarrhea had stopped, but I wasn't getting better. I could hardly stay standing; most of the time I didn't make it to roll call. The other women whispered secretly together and observed with sympathy my mother's efforts to rescue me. They were convinced that my fate had already been decided; each morning they were surprised to see I was still breathing.

February brought rain, and most of the women were coughing and running fevers. Dreadful weeks passed by.

On March 7, in the late hours of the evening, we were called to an extra roll call. "Hurry up, hurry up, out, out!" The cries sounded very nervous, and at first we didn't know what was up. In the darkness we could hear shouting, dogs barking, and orders from all sides.

A few hours earlier we had lain down to sleep, and the light had been turned off. Now, suddenly, Raja was waking me and saying I had to get up and get dressed. I didn't understand why. I noticed the unrest about me, but it didn't interest me; I was somehow beyond it, as if I were suspended in midair.

Raja was pushing me, but no reproaches helped her this time. I couldn't stir myself; I wanted to sleep. Raja began scolding, but she suddenly sensed I was burning with fever. At a loss, she began to dress me herself. She made as much haste as she could in the dark, and I hindered her with all my strength.

We could hear the horrible shouting of the blitz maidens. They were already approaching to hit us when Raja succeeded in getting me up. She supported me so I didn't fall down, and searched for her shoes, which she had lost in the dark. She found them, pulled them on, and took me outside onto the square.

The whole camp was assembled there. In the dark, under a light rain, the roll call began. We were divided into groups, men and women separated.

Raja saw that the groups were slowly beginning to move forward, but when she tried to lead me and get into line, I couldn't walk. Rachel grabbed me on one side, Raja on the other. Together they tried to drag me forward. But my legs wouldn't obey me; it was as if I were crippled.

It was dark and cold. Raja feverishly considered what she could do. She knew from experience that I would fall behind the group after the first few steps, and then . . . She didn't even dare think about it.

Her wounded leg pained her greatly; the wound wasn't healing and had entirely festered. But her feet were also hurting her now. The shoes were pinching her, and she asked herself if they were even hers. Perhaps she had gotten someone else's shoes in the darkness. But she couldn't check that now. Suddenly, a stray beam from a flashlight fell on her feet, and to her astonishment she saw she had put her shoes on the wrong way: the right shoe on the left foot, and vice versa.

In that moment she reached a decision. Convinced she was doing the right thing, she plucked up her courage and turned to one of the blitz maidens. She said the two of us, she and I, were sick and wanted to remain in the camp. The blitz maiden was surprised by her determined request. She tried to explain that a horse wagon had already been ordered for the sick, so that everyone could leave the camp. But Raja, as well as the woman, knew what any exaggerated concern of the Nazis for the sick meant: death.

When another blitz maiden passed by, Raja turned to her and demanded that we be left behind. This one agreed. She ordered us to return to the barracks as quickly as possible.

The train of prisoners began to move. Rachel and Marila, who were standing next to us, said good-bye to us with a long, sad look. It was as though Rachel were asking, How would this chapter end for us? Would we ever start a new page?

We stayed alone on the roll call ground. Raja supported me, and slowly, very slowly, we returned to the barracks.

The whole room was now at our disposal, and there was enough space to lie down. We lay down on the straw. I was burning with fever and took almost no notice of my surroundings anymore. The guard who had been left behind to watch over the camp looked through the open door. Before she lay down, I heard Raja ask the guard, "When will we be shot?"

The young German answered, "I haven't any orders yet. When I get the order to shoot you, then I'll do it." With these words he closed the door.

A few blankets had been left behind. Raja covered me up well and stopped up the cracks in the wall next to me before she lay down beside me. I fell asleep.

The next morning I was somewhat better. The guard brought us a good breakfast from the farmers in the neighborhood: bread, margarine, jam, and tea. At noon we got hot chicken soup with meat, and that evening hot porridge, along with bread and tea again. We ate until we were full.

Each time the guard's footsteps approached our barracks, Raja took my hand to comfort me. Was this the last meal before the order arrived to shoot us? Was he coming this time to let us know he had received "the order"?

But the next day passed quietly, too. We got food and were permitted to rest in the barracks all day long. I slept, woke up sometimes, ate something, and slept again.

A few times Raja went out to the square to see what was going on outside. But other than our guard, nobody appeared to be there any longer. Once, when Raja returned, I was awake. She told me that all the camp inmates had gone. It seemed the two of us were alone. She tried to prepare me for "the end." I was barely reachable; only the good food interested me.

In the evening we heard the roar of cannons and rocket launchers from the front. That night we were wakened by the noise of heavy engines driving on the nearby street, passing our barracks. Raja looked out through the cracks and saw tanks driving through Tauentzien to Lauenburg, in the direction of Gdansk. The earth trembled; the noise was deafening, and gunshots and explosions could be heard from time to time.

When it grew light, Raja recognized the insignias on the military vehicles. They were red stars, and on the caps of the soldiers who sat on the vehicles there were red stars.

It was the Soviet army—our liberators!

Raja left her observation post. Full of joy, she cried, "Susie, the Russians are coming! We are rescued; we are saved, we are liberated, Susie, we are free! Everything is over, Susie, Susinka!"

My mother's words didn't penetrate my consciousness; I heard myself murmuring, "Too bad, today of all days, now that we have a good German guard and are getting enough to eat."

Then I lost consciousness.

223

AS IF
NEWBORN

I ONLY CAME TO a full week after the liberation. In the new life that was opening before me, I was like a child who had just come into the world: without experience, without knowledge, without anything.

When I regained consciousness, I found myself in a soft white bed—a big bed. The white, starched sheets smelled good and pleasant. I lay alone in the bed; I had enough room; nobody was crowding against me. I was clean, washed, and I wore a starched white nightgown.

I closed my eyes and opened them again. Was this all just a dream? A beautiful dream? I lay quietly; I didn't want to move for fear that the wonderful dream would vanish.

I no longer knew what was real. I no longer knew if I was only dreaming this white, comfortable bed, and would soon wake up into terrible reality. Or if I had only dreamed the camp, and now found myself in reality.

Where was I? And where was my mother?

Slowly I opened my eyes again, and looked carefully about the room. It was clean; the ceiling over me was white, and on the white walls hung a pair of framed landscape pictures. Two white rectangular spaces on the wall were empty; a careful hand had taken down two unwanted pictures. What had they been of? Did they conceal a secret?

I propped myself up a bit and looked about me. There were two more large beds in the room; someone seemed to be lying in each of them, covered up with thick blankets. Across from me there was a white door, and on the right a wide window that looked out on a courtyard. The courtyard was big; chickens and geese were roaming about it. I had never seen so many geese in my life. A dog was barking; trees were budding out; nobody could be seen.

I tried to get up, but my legs wouldn't obey me. So I stayed lying down, my head propped on my left arm, enjoying the whiteness and cleanliness about me.

Suddenly everything came back to me. I had really been in the camp, and my mother along with me! Where was she? Why was I alone?

I could no longer lie there quietly; I sat up and looked at the bed that stood to the left of me, against the wall. A strange woman lay there, groaning in pain. A bad smell came from her bed, a smell of rot. I had never seen her before. She was hallucinating, and in her dream she was speaking Hungarian, a language whose sound I recognized from the camp. In order to look at the third bed, which stood beyond mine against the same wall, I would have to get up and take a few steps.

I tried to climb out of bed. My head was swimming. I held on tightly to the bedstead, my legs wobbling. I went forward a few steps. The woman's head was turned to the wall; she lay on the bed without a pillow, and she was covered by a thick featherbed that hid her face. After several efforts I succeeded in advancing to the head of the bed, and suddenly I was trembling. My mother! But how she had changed. Small and shrunken, like a child, she lay in the big bed. Her eyes were closed; her skin was transparent, the mouth and cheeks emaciated. A grizzled child! Was she breathing? What had happened to her? How had we gotten here? I went closer to my mother, leaned myself against her, and tried to wake her up. I wanted to see a sign of life, some proof that she was still breathing!

I was bent over her, lying almost on top of her. After a while I felt her shallow breathing, but I didn't succeed in waking her. I pulled and shook her, but when her eyes finally opened, she didn't look at me. I screamed, but my mother didn't see me; she didn't recognize me.

"Mama, it's me, Susie, Mama, look at me, it's me, your daughter! Mama!" My legs gave out from under me and I fell from her bed to the floor.

After a while a woman came into the room. I didn't know her, and was afraid of her. When she saw me lying on the floor, she immediately called in a young man, who lifted me up and carried me back to my bed.

With trembling heart, I looked at the man who was holding me in his arms. Who was he? What language did he speak? What was he doing here? I was afraid to speak with him. Where was I?

When he noticed that I was conscious, he spoke to me in Polish: "Can you hear me? Can you understand me?"

"Yes," I whispered.

"Don't be afraid! We've been saved! We are free! Free! You've been sick for a long time, very sick, but now you'll get better quickly and go back home! Don't worry; everything will be all right!"

That was hard to believe—and even harder to grasp. Back home? Where should I go back to? Where was I? What was wrong with Raja?

I pointed to the bed next to me, and then I remembered that I wasn't allowed to call her "Mama." He understood my question.

"That woman, there? Do you know her? She is very sick. She will probably soon die; she has only one or two more days at most. It's so sad, that she still has to suffer now."

I cried out. "Mama! Mama! Don't die! Please, don't die! Don't leave me alone!"

The young Pole was startled. He had understood. In order to calm me down, he offered to bring me soup and something to eat.

I stayed in my soft white bed, and I was in complete despair. What should I do? How could I help my mother, how save her? And what would happen to me? Where could I turn; where could I go? Who in the world did I have?

After a short time the young man returned and brought me warm chicken soup with meat in it, and a piece of cake for dessert. He sat down beside me and tried to persuade me to eat. But although hunger was still tormenting me, I was too concerned and agitated to eat anything.

The young Pole said his name was Andrzej, and he told me about himself. While he was talking, he fed me one spoonful of soup after another. He was nineteen, a Pole from Warsaw who had been sent to Stutthof after the big uprising in Warsaw. His father had been killed in the uprising; his mother had remained at home with his little sister.

In the final night, while the prisoners of Tauentzien Camp stood on the square for roll call and another march was being readied, Andrzej had joined a group of Polish men who had decided to stay and not go with the other prisoners.

The Poles knew for certain that the front had advanced close to Gdansk, and they thought it would be better to take the risk and hide in the forest, and wait for liberation, than to take to the road again. The memory of the previous march was seared into them, and they knew the dangers that those on the route would be exposed to. They also didn't want to distance themselves from the front, from the longed-for liberation by the advancing Red Army.

And they succeeded!

In the commotion, the agitation, and the disorder reigning over Tauentzien Camp the night of the evacuation, the guards were unable to hunt out everyone who escaped among the trees and the nearby hills. In that way, several Poles and eight Frenchmen were able to save themselves.

When the young men heard the Red Army approaching, they fell upon the sole guard, beat him to death, and left the camp through the main gates.

After the liberation the Russian army found two other women besides us in the women's barracks. One of them, a young Jewish woman, immediately joined the Red Army and left the camp with them.

We other three stayed in the barracks, feverish and delirious. On the day of the liberation my mother was still conscious. But when the Poles were making sure that we were brought from the barracks to the mayor's beautiful house, she lost consciousness. She was dying.

I was unconscious as well, but my body was in better shape than my mother's.

The third woman had frostbitten legs. Gangrene had set in. Over and over she screamed from the pain, and when she wasn't doing that, she slept. She spoke only Hungarian, and no one understood her.

The freed prisoners made sure that we had been washed and had gotten the biggest and nicest room in the house. Nourishing food was brought to us, but our condition was so bad that we couldn't eat.

I was suffering from spotted typhus, and my mother also came down with typhus one day after we had arrived in this house. The big wound on her right leg—left over from the death march and her fight in the snow for a piece of bread—wasn't healing. On the contrary, the infection was spreading during her illness, and the big, open wound had festered down to the bone. In the whole house there was no medicine or salve that could handle such a badly suppurated wound.

The German residents of the house and the farmers of the neighborhood, who had been forced to care for us, were carrying out their commission unwillingly. They did only the bare minimum. They cooked and brought us food, cleaned the room, and made the beds. We were receiving no medical attention.

Andrzej was the only one caring for us. He was always coming into the room to see if we were eating the food they brought us. He fed us and gave us hot, sweet tea to drink.

Andrzej also told me that the Russian army had pushed through our region very quickly, and had left the enclave in the hands of commissars. The front was advancing forward, and the Russian soldiers were marching toward Berlin. It was the final weeks of the war, and the Russians were concentrating their military strength on the German capital city, on Berlin. The army was drafting everyone who could fight; in their haste, even many who came from the camps. After everything they had survived in the camps, those former prisoners were now marching to Berlin in the ranks of the Red Army.

The state of my health was improving. I had become stronger, and now I could stand up. I sat for hours by my mother and stroked her, brushing the white hair off her forehead. I washed her, tidied and cleaned the vile, stinking wound. I bound up her leg with clean strips of cloth that I had torn from the bedsheets, and tried to feed her. But despite my efforts, her condition was not improving.

I sat there many long hours, crying and begging my mother not to die, not to leave me alone in a world I didn't know. I implored her to tell me what I must do, whom I should seek out, to whom I might turn. But my mother didn't hear me and she didn't recognize me.

Sometimes I went outside to the courtyard, but I was afraid to go any distance from the house. I was afraid my mother might die and that I wouldn't be at her side. Perhaps she'd still wake up for a moment and tell me where I should go, and to whom I should turn. I didn't know the way; I didn't know how far the village was from my hometown of Vilnius. I was all alone.

One night I heard an airplane landing. A big, terrible soldier entered our room. He beamed a flashlight over the beds and stepped back in disgust from the foul odor in the room. He swore in Russian and shouted, "Who are you?"

I answered him in his own language. "We came from the concentration camp on the other side of the forest."

The Russian calmed down and came over to my bed.

"You're just a kid; how could you've been in a camp? Are you Russian?"

"I'm a Jew from Vilnius."

"I'm also a Jew, girl," he said. "I'm a combat pilot. I've just come from my hometown. It's completely ruined; the houses were burned. The Germans killed my entire family. I'm here to take revenge!"

I immediately told him my mother was very sick. We had no medicine and there was no doctor here. My neighbor in the next bed was also very sick; she had frostbitten legs that had been attacked by gangrene; that was the reason for the terrible smell in the room.

The pilot hesitated, then promised to send us help. He asked me the way to the village, and then he went away, after he had promised me to "finish the war soon."

The next day I heard the German women who were attending to us talking about the Russian soldiers who had amused themselves that night in the village. They had trashed houses and raped women.

After a few days a military ambulance came and took our sick neighbor away. They brought various salves for my mother.

I began to treat my mother's leg thoroughly. Every hour, day and night, I cleaned the wound and smeared it with salve. The wound was so deep, I believed I saw the bone. I put pillows under the leg in order to elevate it.

Despite the inexpert treatment, the wound began to heal, and hope awoke in me that my mother would survive. The young men were expecting her to die any minute, but I firmly believed that as long as she was still alive, she had a chance to get healthy.

A few times a day I went to the henhouse, looked for fresh eggs, and drank them on the spot, just like that. Sometimes they were still lukewarm.

I began to eat a lot. Andrzej warned me not to overdo it, since my body was not yet accustomed to lots of nourishment. Two Poles had died after liberation by eating too much at one go. Their bodies hadn't been in a condition to digest so much food, after years of starvation.

I was tall for my age, but I weighed only about thirty kilograms (sixty-six pounds). My arms and my legs were long and crooked, my head was small on my long, thin, body. The great amount of food didn't harm me. But I suffered terrible pain in my legs. I often cried from the pain, and was unable to move. My legs hurt especially at night. I often woke up from the pain, and then I would whimper for hours.

I was having nightmares. Over and over pictures appeared before my eyes of the ghetto and the camp, of the death march and the voyage on the ship, of the roll calls and the dreadful night we spent outside, naked, after our disinfection. Then I would wake up screaming, not knowing where I was.

One night I woke myself with my own loud crying; I had once more had bad dreams. Because my legs were hurting especially badly that night, I didn't stop crying. The pain and the despair were overwhelming me, and I began crying into the night with all my strength.

Suddenly I heard a quiet voice calling my name; it was the voice of my mother! I couldn't believe my ears. Was I only imagining I was hearing her voice? Was I still asleep?

I immediately fell silent, and in the quiet, I heard my mother's voice whispering, "Susinka, Susinka, what's the matter? Don't cry, please don't cry, be quiet."

I sat up in the darkness and noticed that my mother was inching toward me in her bed. I sprang up, ran over to her, and took her in my arms. We both cried for joy, and neither of us could utter a word.

Two days later came the news of the war's end.

We were happy. The Poles came to our room and we congratulated one another. They brought us presents— clothes and sweets they had taken away from the houses of the Germans in the neighborhood.

My mother got well slowly. It was a long and difficult time. Again and again she would lose awareness and become unconscious; I could awaken her only with difficulty. When she was awake, she could no longer remember the past, and had forgotten everything that had happened to her. She had forgotten her house in Vilnius and her family, and she was behaving like a small child. I had to show her how to eat, because she had forgotten how to use a knife and fork. I taught her to dress herself, to walk, to wash herself. Bit by bit her memory returned. By the time she first sat down to eat at the table, she could remember that she had drunk tea from a samovar in her father's house. And so she gradually acquired all her memories again.

Her appearance continued to scare me. This woman, who had once been so beautiful, was forty-one and looked seventy. She was very small and shriveled and weighed thirty-three kilograms (seventy-three pounds). Her legs and arms were thin and hung down from her; her face was small, and only her eyes were alive. Her cheekbones stuck out. It was difficult to find clothes in her size; her body had the dimensions of a child's, and every dress the young Poles brought her hung off her as if from a clothes rack.

The Russian military administration was beginning to gather the survivors of the area in order to transport them to the Soviet Union. I wanted to go back quickly to Vilnius, for I was hoping to find relatives there. Therefore, I proposed we should join the transport. My mother refused. Because Vilnius had been annexed to the Soviet Union, we would be considered Soviet citizens. The authorities wanted us taken to the Soviet Union. They promised us that there we would be taken to a collective farm. But my mother explained to the officials that she could serve the Soviet Union much better here, rather than working on a collective farm. She understood that we would soon have to leave the area and return to Vilnius our own way if we were not to fall back into the hands of deportations and camps.

A young man traveling to the region's main city, Lębork, brought us each back identification papers. My mother and I were dismayed by the appearance of the papers we received. The original text had been changed. "Ob," the abbreviation for "citizen," had been crossed out, and replaced by the word "Jewess" ("Żydówka").* This, after all that we and the Jews of Europe had been through! We looked at the pass and found it tough to understand the ignorance of the officials who had issued such a certificate.

At the beginning of July my mother was strong enough to be capable of traveling back to Vilnius. We began our preparations. The Poles too were ready to go home. They proposed we join them for the first leg of the trip.

They brought us suitcases they had confiscated from the Germans, and we filled them with our clothes and with food, because we feared there might not be enough to eat in Poland. Andrzej had found pretty pink wool, and my mother knitted a little dress for his sister, a present that made Andrzej proud and happy.

We set out with our suitcases full of canned foods. Our new acquaintances, the young men from the camp, accompanied us. They also helped us board an overcrowded train heading for Warsaw.

Poland had been destroyed, and the train advanced

---

* See the document on next page.

**Starosta Powiatowy
w Leborku**

Nr. rej. 2~~55~~ 45

Przepustka. *Nr. Lagru.*
95383.

~~Żydówka.~~) *Wcksler Zuzanna*

ur *14. 11. 1932.* w *Paris*

zam *Talencyn pow. Lębork*

udaje się do *Wilna*

i zpowrotem. W celach *Powrót z lagru*

na stare miejsce zamieszkania

Wszelkie władze uprasza się wymienionemu(nej) nie
czynić żadnych trudności w podrozy.
Niniejsza przepustka ważna jest do dn *15. 7. 45.*

Starosta Powiatowy

Lębork, dn *15. 5.* 1945. *JNowakowski*

Opłatę administracyjna pobrano

w kwocie *—* złotych.

N. N. Z. 4.45.

laboriously between the ruined towns and villages. After three days we reached Warsaw, the capital city.

Andrzej parted from us and hurried home. He promised to meet us at the train station in the Praga district. There we would take a train that went toward the Russian border, in the direction of Vilnius.

We rented a horse wagon, and together with the other travelers, we picked our way through the ruined streets of the city. Debris and wreckage lay everywhere, and our driver often had to climb down and move stones out of the way. The bridge over the Vistula River had been blown up. A long line of horse-drawn wagons and people with loaded baby carriages stood at the interim wooden bridge, in order to get to the other side of the river. We waited for hours, until it was our turn; in the meantime street vendors came by selling drinks, sweets, and other things.

Suddenly I saw fresh bread—white, shining little rolls. I was only with great difficulty able to swallow the saliva that flooded into my mouth. I couldn't tear my eyes away from those rolls; they seemed to beckon to me. Until then I had eaten only the black bread we had brought with us from Tauentzien. My mother saw how I was yearning, and said, "I'm afraid we don't have any money for that."

I was silent; she was too. But she would have done everything possible to satisfy my craving and buy me the bread. So she took the shawl from around her throat and offered it in exchange for the little rolls. She got four of them. My mother gave me one of the little loaves, and I held it carefully in my hands and breathed in the wonderful smell. Then I took a piece of black bread and began to eat: a big bite of bread and—as the meat in the sandwich, so to speak—a little bite of the roll. What a treat! My mother was laughing and crying by turns.

When we got to the train station in Praga, the driver unloaded our suitcases and let all the passengers out. My

235

mother and I stood there with four big, heavy suitcases. We picked them up and went forward, but after a couple of steps we had to put them down and rest. Filled with food—primarily canned goods—our suitcases were much too heavy for us, thin and weak as we were. We couldn't take more than a few steps. But suddenly, to our joy, two men came and offered us their help. We held on to only the small parcels in our hands, and pushed through the crowd, following the two men carrying our suitcases. But the men were walking very fast, and after a while they disappeared from our sight into the crowd.

We stood on the train platform and we no longer had anything—only our handbags and the small parcels . . . and of course the rolls!

We climbed aboard the train and found seats. And then we saw Andrzej, who was looking for us. He had come, as he had promised, but there were tears in his eyes, and his face was sad and sunken. He gave us the news that his mother and sister had been killed in a bombardment in the final days before the liberation of Warsaw.

When our train started up, Andrzej stayed back on the platform, alone and unhappy. Before we parted, he gave back to my mother the pretty little dress she had knitted for his sister. We didn't know how we could comfort him.

On the train to Vilnius we met Jews who explained to us that the border between Poland and the Soviet Union now ran between the former Polish cities of Bialystok and Grodno. They advised us to remain in Bialystok, and not to cross the border. Many people coming from the west didn't reach their destinations, but were sent directly from the border to Siberia. At any rate, it would be impossible for us to return from Vilnius to Poland. It would be more sensible to remain in a city near the border and to wait for news. Perhaps we would even find relatives there.

We got out in Bialystok and rented a shabby, cheap

room from a poor family. My mother found work in a recla-
mation center for recycling trash such as paper, glass, and
metal. She earned hardly enough for bread, milk, yogurt,
and sometimes a couple of beers. I often roamed about the
marketplace. I was selling the trifles we had in our small
parcels: wool for knitting, socks, hairpins, and so on. My
shoes were wearing out; my clothes were ragged; and winter was coming on.

THE AUTHOR WITH HER MOTHER
BIALYSTOK, SPRING 1946

My mother went to the train station each day in hopes of meeting someone she knew, or getting news of friends or relatives. One day she met a man she recognized from Vilnius. He said he knew that Wolodja was still alive; they had been together during the death march and at the liberation. We were always glad when we met someone from the old days; now we naturally also hoped that Wolodja was really still living. My mother wrote our address on a piece of paper. She gave it to the man and invited him to visit us in Bialystok.

November 14, 1945, was my thirteenth birthday, the first one after the liberation. My mother tried to make the day a little festive for me. To celebrate, there was a sort of homemade eggnog; it was the first time I ever drank something like that. After the meal my mother crossed the courtyard; she had to use the toilet, and it was in the garden.

Suddenly she heard someone at the fence trying to open the gate. It was a dangerous period. Criminals and thieves were roaming throughout the city. Discharged soldiers were breaking into homes, raping women, and stealing the little that they found. And groups from the "Armia Krajowa," the Polish anti-Soviet underground, were waylaying peaceful citizens, especially Jews, robbing them, and beating them up.

My mother was frightened and she listened tensely. She heard the sound of a Dynamo flashlight being switched on.

My mother was startled. Before the war Julek had always used just such a flashlight. Loudly she asked, *"Kto tam?"* Who's there?

"Raja, Raja!" cried the Russian soldier who had finally succeeded in opening the gate and entering.

At once my mother recognized the voice of her brother, and cried, "Wolodja, it's you!" Completely distraught, she left her brother standing in the courtyard, ran through the kitchen door into the house, and shouted, "Susinka,

Wolodja's here!" Then she ran back to open the front door on the other side of the apartment.

My knees gave out. My legs turned to water. I fell on the floor and couldn't get up. I heard the apartment door opening, and then the voice of my uncle Wolodja.

"Where is Susie?"

On my stomach, I crawled through all the rooms to the front door. It was the best present I could have received for my birthday. Wolodja picked me up off the floor and sat me down on a chair beside him. He had brought presents and sugar with him. I hadn't seen or tasted any sugar for a long time. Out of sheer delight, I ate the sugar with a soup-spoon.

Later we sat together and recounted what we had lived through since we had last seen each other in Stutthof.

WOLODJA'S
STORY

IN JANUARY 1945 Julek and Wolodja, as well as Wolodja's brother-in-law and father-in-law, had been put into one of the columns that was leaving Stutthof. They began their death march on January 25 with the fifth group setting out that day, together with Poles, Russians, Italians, Germans, and a group of Jewish prisoners. All in all, eleven hundred men. The bodily condition of the men in this group was comparatively good; they reached their scheduled sleeping place the first day. There, a bitter surprise was awaiting them. The barn that was to serve them overnight was occupied by the fourth column, which had set out too late and had been held up on the way. The authorities of the fifth column could find no sleeping place for the prisoners and took them to a small nearby forest. There they passed the night on the frozen ground, among trees and bushes. The next morning they got neither food nor anything warm to drink.

On the second day of the march the men were weak and exhausted. Hungry and thirsty as they were, they advanced slowly. That evening they found no shelter. They had to pass the night out in the open once more.

The third day of their march was especially hard. The weather had deteriorated; it began snowing, and the groups lost their way and got stuck in deep snow. That evening they found shelter in a barn, and there they received something to eat for the first time. Wolodja's brother-in-law became ill; he coughed and ran a high fever. Chassia's father,

Wolodja's father-in-law, was very weak and could walk only with great difficulty. But Julek's condition was the worst. His feet were frostbitten; his shoes were falling apart. During the night his feet warmed up; they swelled, became red, and hurt him badly. Because of the pain, Julek couldn't sleep for a minute. Next morning he begged them to leave him behind in the barn. He couldn't stand it any longer. But Wolodja helped him to wrap his swollen feet in rags and paper. He tried to stop up the holes in his shoes, and he persuaded Julek to go on, for soon their suffering would be ended, and they would be freed. But after they had gone a few kilometers (a mile or two), the holes in Julek's shoes broke open again; the paper got wet, and the rags Wolodja had wrapped about his feet fell apart. Julek was dragging himself through the snow with naked, frostbitten toes. That day he wanted to simply stop and let the group pass him by, so that his suffering could be brought to an end. But Wolodja wouldn't let him give up.

But the going became harder and harder for Julek. The next night they came to a barn whose walls had been damaged and were letting in snow and wind. It was an especially cold night, and the snow that swirled in melted, leaving straw and clothing wet. Julek's frostbitten feet were full of blisters; many of the blisters burst, and pus ran out of the wounds.

The next morning Julek could stand up on his painful feet only with the greatest difficulty. They hurt him so badly, he could hardly fit them into his ragged shoes. He must have been certain that he would have to fight with Wolodja if he asked him to leave him behind in the barn. And so he gathered all his strength together and set out with the others, despite his horrible pain. On that day it was again snowing very heavily.

The men had wrapped themselves in blankets; they moved like shadows or ghosts along the road. Julek was walking in a row with Wolodja. His shoes were rubbing against his wounded feet. The open wounds were unbearably painful. Julek didn't want to go on, but Wolodja and his brother-in-law held him tightly and supported him. When the column started up again after a short rest by the side of the road, Julek hid among other men. He stood up only when Wolodja had already passed a few rows ahead. Wolodja was gazing about for him, and when he spotted him in one of the five-man rows behind him, he stayed back in order to let him catch up. But Julek saw him, and so he also stopped for a moment. So several more rows passed him, and he was putting more and more distance between himself and Wolodja. All this time Wolodja was trying to reach Julek before he fell behind the column. Wolodja stopped and let a few more rows pass him by, in hopes of getting to Julek faster, in order to take him by the arm and pull him onward.

The sad game between the two men went on for about ten minutes or more. Wolodja would walk on a ways, and then stop and try to reach Julek; at the same time, he was taking care that the German guards didn't catch on to what was happening.

With a final effort Julek tried disappearing among the men and getting as far away from Wolodja as possible. By the time Wolodja had almost reached him, Julek was already in the last row. Wolodja stood still, in order to wait for that row to catch up to him. This was the boundary. After that row went by, there would be no more saving him. But when the final row got to Wolodja, he didn't succeed in grabbing Julek by the hand, because Julek had once again stopped—this time behind the whole column, alone.

Wolodja shouted, trying to rouse Julek's will to live, but Julek froze to the spot and didn't move. To fall behind the column was suicide. The group marched on and Wolodja went with it, but he continued to shout and call Julek, with his head turned backward. Julek's figure disappeared in the snowy field. Wolodja heard the gunshot and knew that Julek Rauch, his brother-in-law, had been killed at that moment. The next day his father-in-law died. He fell asleep at night, in the church in which they were staying over, and he never woke up.

Wolodja's group arrived in one of the villages near Lauenburg; in other words, not very far from Tauentzien. They stayed there under the most horrible conditions, sick and hungry. His brother-in-law fell sick with typhus and died at the end of February. When he learned that the Red Army was advancing nearer, Wolodja fled into the forest with a couple of other men. A few days later, on the tenth of March, he was liberated by the Russian army.

Although starved and weakened, Wolodja was one of the few who had stayed healthy. In the first days after the liberation, he helped his sick friends and scavenged for food and medicine.

One week after the liberation, additional Russian units arrived in the village. The former prisoners welcomed them with great joy and affection, but the commissar of the soldiers was a harsh and mistrustful man. He wrote down the names of those rescued on a list, and he had a doctor examine those who were sick. The commissar inquired about the place of origin of each man. When he heard that Wolodja came from Vilnius, he immediately listed him as a Russian citizen. He was surprised that a Jew had succeeded in saving himself. Up to then he hadn't met any Jews who had survived a concentration camp. Wolodja appeared healthier than the other prisoners, and so the commissar came to suspect that Wolodja had perhaps collaborated with the Germans. And so he decided, "You're joining the Red Army. You'll fight against the Germans, and thereby justify your survival."

On the sixth day after being liberated from the concentration camp, Wolodja was drafted into the Red Army. After only two days' training he was sent to the front to fight against the Germans.

Wolodja pushed on with the troops until they reached Berlin. He stayed there until the end of October; then he was ordered to go to the Soviet Union to be demobilized from the army.

With a big group of soldiers from the front, he traveled by train through liberated Europe: through Germany and Poland, toward Vilnius.

The train could advance only slowly, and Wolodja was very excited; he was still hoping to find some of the family alive. Wherever the train halted, the soldiers thronged to the windows and looked out, shouting and conversing with the natives.

At a train station shortly before Warsaw, his military train stopped right beside a train of civilian travelers. The civilians and the soldiers scrutinized each other. The windows were open, and the trains stood so close to each other that the passengers could touch one another. They struck up conversations, offered each other cigarettes, inquired about this and that, and wished one another the best.

When the train with the civilian passengers was already in motion, Wolodja suddenly heard someone calling his name. He rushed to the window and noticed someone he recognized from Vilnius and from the camps. He was happy to see him.

The man was waving at Wolodja with something he held in his hand, but in the overall commotion it was impossible to understand a word. Then, a small paper ball flew through Wolodja's window. The train moved on. Wolodja unwrapped the paper, and on it he found an address in the handwriting of his sister, Raja—our address in Bialystok.

Wolodja traveled farther on the train, his heart full of hope. Happiness and impatience to see his sister filled him.

He roamed restlessly from one car to the next, and inquired again and again about the train stops. Out of fear of missing Bialystok, he didn't dare go to sleep. Besides that, he was looking for a way to leave the train, since it was forbidden for soldiers to get out. Somehow, he managed it.

And so he had come to us, tired and without strength, dressed in a Russian uniform. Wolodja had changed greatly since we had last seen him. He was thirty-five years old, but he reminded me of my grandfather, who had been seventy. His back was bent, his face shriveled, and the little hair that remained at his temples had turned white. His smile was sad, and even his eyes had lost their earlier merriment and were dim. The concentration camp had made an impotent, despondent man of him.

As a soldier he had tried to learn something about us and the fate of the women from Stutthof. He had heard the women from there had been taken away: most on the death march, some by small ships on the sea route. The ships had been sunk, either by the Germans or by air attacks. He had inquired about the fate of the women who had taken part in the death march, and had learned that only a small number had succeeded in staying alive. Wolodja also told us of the bitter fate of the prisoners who had left Tauentzien the night before the liberation. A small number of them had been freed on the way; Rachel was among them. The other women had managed to reach Stutthof, but there the poor wretches had been bundled onto ships, which had been blown up on the high seas. So it had come full circle. Stutthof was liberated on May 8, 1945, the day the war ended.

I loved my uncle, and my relationship with him was very close. He also loved me and found in me a kind of substitute for the loved ones he had lost. He often spoke with me about his wife, Chassia, and especially about his daughter, Fejgele, both of whom had been killed. He became for me a caring father, and above all, he helped me find my bearings in the new life that now began for us: a life in freedom.

After some time we learned from people who had returned from Vilnius that Jechiel, Julia, and Jochele Tejschew had been betrayed to the Gestapo for "bounty money" by the farmers in Puszkarnia. They had been taken by surprise while working in the fields near the Puszkarnia farm, and shot on the spot.

Dora, my mother's cousin, had succeeded in fleeing from the train and returning to Vilnius. She never found her son, Lonja. Since she found no hiding place on the Aryan side, in her despair, she slipped into the Kailis labor camp. She met my father's brother, Schneior, there.

Schneior had fled from Rossa, from the transport that was going to Estonia, and had returned to Vilnius in hopes of finding his wife, Schejndl, and his daughter, Sarele Weksler. But they had gone to the left, and wound up in the extermination camp of Majdanek.

Schneior and Dora stayed together until a few days before the liberation of Vilnius. Two days before the city's liberation the Germans had liquidated the Kailis labor camp. Schneior and Dora were still trying to hide, but they had been discovered and were shot on the square of the camp.

Out of our entire family, only we three remained:

My uncle, Wolodja; my mother, Raja; and I, Susie Weksler.

THE AUTHOR
IN BIALYSTOK, SPRING 1946

SCHOSCHANA RABINOVICI, 1990
VISITING KAISERWALD

SCHOSCHANA RABINOVICI

Schoschana Rabinovici was born Susanne Weksler on November 14, 1932, in Paris, where her parents were living while pursuing their studies. In 1937 her parents returned to Vilnius, where Schoschana attended the Jewish school.

She survived the war, in the ghetto and in various concentration camps.

Of her large family, only an uncle, her mother, and she survived.

After the war, Schoschana Rabinovici went to Polish schools in Bialystok and Lodz. In 1950 she emigrated to Israel.

In 1952 she fulfilled her military service. In the following year she married David Rabinovici (pronounced *Rabinovitch*). Her two sons were born in 1955 and 1961. She lives with her family in Tel Aviv and, since 1964, also in Vienna.